JAMES TANNER
takes 5

JAMES TANNER

takes

DELICIOUS DISHES USING JUST 5 INGREDIENTS

PHOTOGRAPHY BY
ANDERS SCHØNNEMANN

KYLE CATHIE LIMITED

I would like to dedicate this book to my daughter Megan.

Big thanks to Kyle Cathie for letting me do the book, Sophie Allen for putting it all together, Nicky Collings for styling and layout, Anders Schønnemann for his great photography, Karen Taylor for food styling, Becca Watson for recipe testing and Liz Belton for prop styling. My Big Bro Chris Tanner for holding the fort whilst we were shooting the pics, Sianypie Lane for typing up all my scribbles and Big Gav for being Big Gav.

Also all the boys and girls from Tanners Restaurant and Barbican Kitchen who inspire me in their special moments....

First published in Great Britain in 2010 by
Kyle Cathie Limited
www.kylecathie.com

ISBN 978 1 85626 917 9

A Cataloguing in Publication record for this title is available from the British Library.

10 9 8 7 6 5 4 3 2 1

James Tanner hereby identified as the authors of this work in accordance with Section 77 of the Copyright, Designs and Patents Act 1988.

Text copyright © 2010 James Tanner
Design © 2010 Kyle Cathie Limited
Photography © 2010 Anders Schønnemann

Design Nicky Collings
Photography Anders Schønnemann
Project Editor Sophie Allen
Food stylist Karen Taylor
Props stylist Liz Belton
Copy editor Stephanie Evans
Production Gemma John

Colour reproduction by Sang Choy
Printed by C&C Offset Printing Co.

Contents

INTRODUCTION

Welcome to **James Tanner Takes 5**, a collection of delectable recipes for the home cook, each using just five ingredients in addition to three store-cupboard staples: oil, sea salt and black pepper. I've included something for everyone and for every occasion, from a quick meal to an elaborate feast, from fish to meat, vegetables to desserts. This collection draws on the dishes I have cooked, served and eaten in my home, on holiday, and in restaurants that I have worked in, and it is a book that can be used every day to prepare wonderful, inspirational food.

Whenever you are cooking, for yourself or other people, both the cooking and the eating experience should be enjoyable. **Takes 5** removes the pressure from shopping for or preparing long lists of ingredients that might be difficult to find or are seldom used, and lets you concentrate on creating great-tasting food without the stress.

If you're already an enthusiastic home cook, I have added some tips to encourage you to experiment: use these recipes and add your own twist. After all, cooking is about being creative with and inspired by ingredients and flavours. Some are pure classics, some are not! I have researched my much-loved favourites and pared them down to create bold, big-flavour food using five ingredients that are easy to buy in your local stores and markets.

My key recommendations when looking for ingredients is to think in terms of quality and seasonality. Try to buy the best you can afford and buy your produce when it's at its best – locally, if possible. Well grown and reared food speaks volumes in flavour, and taste is what it is all about!

So sit back, relax and choose something you're going to love to cook – you're only five ingredients away from a delicious dish!

James Tanner x

Little Dishes

These recipes are fantastic for a light lunch, brunch, simple snack or a starter.

CHILLED MELON & AVOCADO SOUP

This is a palate-cleansing soup that is refreshing on a hot summer's day. Smooth melon, rich avocado and zesty citrus teamed with a dollop of crème fraîche and a few raspberries to top it off. Serve this seriously chilled!

Serves 4

1 ripe avocado, **halved and stoned**
1 melon **(galia or cantaloupe)**
500ml freshly squeezed orange juice
4 tablespoons crème fraîche
12 ripe raspberries

Put the avocado halves cut-side down on a flat surface and score the skin with a sharp knife. Peel the skin back to remove. Discard the skin and roughly chop the avocado.

Cut the melon in half, deseed and scoop out the flesh. Place the melon flesh in a liquidiser or food-processor with the avocado and orange juice and blend to a smooth cream. Pass through a fine sieve. Chill the soup for an hour before serving and, at the same time, chill four soup bowls.

Ladle the soup into chilled soup bowls and serve with a rounded dessert-spoonful of crème fraiche and a sprinkling of raspberries in each bowl.

SPICED PARSNIP SOUP WITH BRAMLEY APPLE

Parsnips, spicey cumin and tart apple make a great warming combination.

Serves 4

2 teaspoons cumin seeds
2 tablespoons olive oil
2 onions, **roughly chopped**
700g parsnips, **peeled and sliced**
1 litre good chicken stock
175g (1 medium) bramley apple, **peeled, cored and grated**
crushed sea salt and freshly ground black pepper

Heat a non-stick frying pan over a high heat for 1 minute. Add the cumin seeds. Reduce the heat and dry roast the seeds for 2 minutes until toasted. Remove from the heat and crush using a pestle and mortar.

Heat the olive oil in a large pan, add the onions and cook for 5 minutes over a low heat until softened but not coloured. Add the parsnips and crushed cumin seeds. Cover the pan with a lid and cook over a low heat for 15–20 minutes, stirring occasionally, until the parsnips are just starting to soften.

In a separate pan, bring the chicken stock to the boil. Pour the hot stock over the parsnips and bring to the boil.

Pour into a liquidiser or food-processor and blend until smooth (you may have to do this in batches). Season with crushed sea salt and freshly ground black pepper.

When ready to serve, return the soup to a clean pan, stir in the grated apple and cook over a low heat for 3 minutes. Ladle the soup into warmed bowls.

CARROT & CORIANDER SOUP

Fresh carrots, a touch of coriander – simplicity in a pot.

Serves 4

15g (handful) fresh coriander
   leaves, chopped, plus a few
   leaves for garnish

1 tablespoon olive oil

1 onion, finely chopped

1 teaspoon coriander seeds,
   crushed

450g carrots, peeled and thinly
   sliced

850ml vegetable stock (made
   with Marigold swiss vegetable
   bouillon powder)

crushed sea salt

Heat the olive oil in a large heavy-based pan. Add the onion and coriander seeds, stirring to combine. Cover with a lid and cook over a low heat for 5 minutes, stirring occasionally until softened but not coloured. Add the carrots, cover and cook over a low heat for a further 15–20 minutes, stirring occasionally, until just starting to soften.

In a separate pan, bring the vegetable stock to the boil. Pour over the carrots and bring to the boil.

Pour into a liquidiser or food-processor and blend until smooth (you may have to do this in batches). Season with crushed sea salt.

When ready to serve, return the soup to a clean pan, stir in the chopped coriander (reserving a few leaves for garnish) and reheat gently. Ladle the soup into warmed bowls. Top with the reserved coriander leaves.

FRENCH ONION SOUP

This soup takes some time to cook. The onions need to be cooked slowly to release their natural sugars, but it's well worth the wait. Of course, it is a real classic with the accompaniment of gruyère croûtons.

Serves 4

50g butter

2 tablespoons olive oil

1kg onions, thinly sliced

1 bay leaf

small bunch fresh thyme (tied
   with string), plus extra leaves
   for garnish

1 litre good beef stock

crushed sea salt and freshly
   ground black pepper

Heat the butter and olive oil in a large heavy-based pan until the butter has melted. Add the onions, reduce the heat, cover and gently cook for 20 minutes until softened but not coloured. Shake the pan occasionally to prevent the onions from sticking to the base.

Increase the heat slightly, add the bay leaf and bunch of tied thyme and cook, covered, for a further 20 minutes until the onions are dark golden, sticky and caramelised. Stir occasionally to prevent the onions from sticking to the base.

Add the stock, stirring with a wooden spoon, scraping the base of the pan well. Bring to the boil, reduce the heat and simmer on a very low heat for 20 minutes. Remove the bunch of thyme and discard. Skim off any fat from the top of the pan and season with crushed sea salt and freshly ground black pepper.

Ladle into warmed bowls and garnish with fresh thyme leaves.

WATERCRESS SOUP

This is no ordinary soup. When I was first shown how to make this, it was drilled into me that the soup had to taste fantastic with perfect seasoning but also to be the perfect colour. Part of catching that colour is quick cooking – if you are not serving it straightaway, you can save the gorgeous bright green by rapidly chilling the soup. The soup can be served hot or cold and is also great served with a poached egg.

Serves 4

250g (2 bunches) watercress, washed
2 tablespoons olive oil
2 onions, finely chopped
2 garlic cloves, peeled and crushed
1 potato, peeled and thinly sliced
850ml chicken stock
crushed sea salt and freshly ground black pepper

Pick the stems from the watercress and finely chop. Set aside the watercress leaves. Heat the olive oil in a heavy-based pan. Add the onions and garlic and cook over a low heat for 5 minutes, stirring occasionally until softened but not coloured. Add the sliced potato and chopped watercress stalks to the pan and cook for a further 10 minutes until the potatoes are soft.

In a separate pan, bring the chicken stock to the boil. Pour over the potato and onion mixture. Add half the watercress leaves and bring to the boil.

Pour into a liquidiser or food-processor with the remaining watercress leaves and blend until smooth (you may have to do this in batches). Season with crushed sea salt and freshly ground black pepper. Pass through a fine sieve into a heatproof bowl sat in a bowl of iced water.

When ready to serve, return the soup to a clean pan and reheat gently. Ladle the soup into warmed bowls.

FENNEL, ORANGE, POMEGRANATE & PECORINO SALAD

Such a simple salad with clean, fresh flavours. Great for accompanying a meal eaten in the garden on a warm day.

Serves 4

2 large fennel bulbs, trimmed
4 tablespoons olive oil
juice of 1 lemon
4 large blood oranges, peeled and segmented
150g pack of pomegranate seeds or seeds from 4 halved pomegranates
150g pecorino
crushed sea salt and freshly ground black pepper

Using a mandolin or sharp knife, slice the fennel very (paper) thinly.

Place the fennel in a bowl, add the olive oil and lemon juice and toss together.

Add the blood orange segments and pomegranate seeds. Season with crushed sea salt and freshly ground black pepper and toss together.

Arrange the fennel salad on serving plates and use a vegetable peeler to shave the pecorino over the top of each plate.

TIP
To avoid getting that chewy taste of the thin skin (membrane) between each orange segment, remove the peel and then use a small paring knife to cut between the membrane of each segment. They should come away cleanly.

BAKED BEETROOT & GOAT'S CHEESE STACKS

Beetroot and goat's cheese are great together: the earthy taste of roasted beets marries perfectly with creamy rich goat's cheese and the balsamic vinegar in the dressing adds a bit of zing. Serve with lamb's lettuce for a touch of green.

Serves 4

3 large beetroots, washed but unpeeled

2 tablespoons olive oil, plus extra for oiling

200g british goat's cheese (choose a semi-dried log)

100ml whipping cream

1 shallot, finely chopped

1 tablespoon balsamic vinegar

crushed sea salt and freshly ground black pepper

Preheat the oven to 200°C/400°F/gas mark 6. Oil the beetroot and place on a large sheet of foil. Sprinkle with crushed sea salt. Gather the edges of the foil together to seal the beetroot in a foil parcel. Bake for 1 hour. Remove from the oven, unwrap the foil and leave the beetroot to cool.

Crumble the goat's cheese into the bowl of a food-processor. Season with crushed sea salt and freshly ground black pepper and pulse until blended. Add the whipping cream and blitz until just smooth. Spoon the goat's cheese mixture into a piping bag fitted with a plain nozzle.

Peel the cooled beetroot and cut into 1cm slices (you need 4 slices from each beetroot). Using a 6cm pastry cutter, cut the beetroot slices into discs, reserving the trimmings. Pipe a small amount of goat's cheese mixture onto the centre of four serving plates and top each with a beetroot disc. Pipe more goat's cheese on top of the beetroot discs and continue layering the beetroot and goat's cheese until you have a stack of 3 discs of beetroot on each plate.

Chop the reserved beetroot trimmings and place in a bowl with the shallot.

Stir in the olive oil and balsamic vinegar and season with crushed sea salt and freshly ground black pepper. Drizzle around the beetroot and goats cheese stacks and serve.

MUSHROOM & GOAT'S CHEESE PARCELS

Juicy baked mushrooms, creamy goat's cheese and pungent pesto, finished off with crisp puff pastry make this recipe a real winner!

Serves 4

4 large field (Portobello) mushrooms

olive oil, for brushing

150g goat's cheese

4 teaspoons pesto

1 free-range egg yolk, **beaten**

375g packet ready-rolled puff pastry

crushed sea salt and freshly ground black pepper

Preheat the oven to 220°C/425°F/gas mark 7. Wipe the mushrooms with kitchen paper, remove the stalk and discard. Oil the caps of the mushrooms and place on a baking tray, gill-side up. Season with crushed sea salt and freshly ground black pepper.

Crumble the goat's cheese into a small bowl and sprinkle some over each mushroom. Spoon one teaspoon of pesto on top of the goat's cheese.

Unroll the pastry on to a lightly floured surface. Lightly roll out the pastry to form a 30cm square. Cut the square into four squares measuring 15cm.

Brush the edges of the pastry squares with beaten egg and place one square of pastry, egg-side down, over each mushroom. Press the pastry around and under the mushroom caps to seal.

Score the top of the pastry in a criss-cross pattern. Brush with beaten egg and bake for 16–18 minutes until the pastry is golden brown. Remove from the oven and leave to stand for 2 minutes before serving.

TIP
You could fill these parcels with lots of different combinations of flavours. Just make sure the filling isn't too 'wet' or the pastry will become soggy.

BAKED CAMEMBERT WITH THYME & GARLIC

This recipe is a favourite of mine on a cold winter's night as it always reminds me of times with friends when we would ski and snowboard all day then sit by a log fire and eat and drink all night. If you don't have maple syrup to hand use a spoonful of honey instead.

Serves 4

- 1 x 250g camembert in its wooden box
- 1 garlic clove, peeled and sliced into matchsticks
- ½ teaspoon fresh thyme leaves
- 1 tablespoon maple syrup
- 1 small baguette, cut into 0.5cm slices
- 2 tablespoons olive oil, plus extra for brushing
- crushed sea salt

Preheat the oven to 200°C/400°F/gas mark 6. Remove the camembert from the box and discard any wax paper packaging. Take a 25cm square of foil and place in the box. Place the camembert inside.

Pierce the top of the camembert with the point of a knife and push in the slices of garlic. Sprinkle over the thyme leaves and drizzle over the maple syrup. Loosely scrunch the foil up over the cheese. Set aside.

Brush two 30cm square sheets (the size of your baking sheet) of baking parchment with oil. Line a baking sheet with one of the oiled parchment sheets, oil-side up. Spread the slices of baguette over the sheet. Drizzle with olive oil and sprinkle with crushed sea salt. Place the remaining sheet of parchment, oil-side down, over the bread.

Place in the oven with the camembert and cook both for 10–12 minutes until the cheese has risen and the bread is crisp. Open up the foil and dip in the hot baguette for a simple supper. Delicious!

ROAST PEARS, BLUE CHEESE FONDUE & WALNUTS

A twist on a fondue using classic ingredients that have been served together for years. This particular recipe works well with a simple green salad.

Serves 4

1 teaspoon olive oil
4 ripe but firm pears (conference), peeled, cored and halved
100ml white wine
180g blue cheese (devon blue)
1 tablespoon blossom honey
50g walnut pieces, toasted

Preheat the oven to 180°C/350°F/gas mark 4. Heat the olive oil in a deep non-stick frying pan. Cook the halved pears over a medium heat for 2 minutes on each side. Remove from the pan and arrange in a 20cm square gratin dish.

Add the white wine to the pan that the pears were in. Add the blue cheese and honey and stir over a low heat until the cheese has melted to a fondue.

Spoon the blue cheese fondue over the pears and roast in the oven for 15–20 minutes until golden and bubbling. Leave to stand for 2 minutes. Spoon the pears into warmed serving dishes and sprinkle with the toasted walnuts.

TIP
You could use apples instead of pears – try English Cox or Braeburn. And of course you can vary the blue cheese as to how strong you like your cheese.

EGGS FLORENTINE

This classic dish reminds me of my catering college days. The recipe is a simple version that can be created in minutes. Make sure your spinach is well washed and dried before cooking and that the eggs are runny when served! Why not serve with a English muffin to create a vegetarian Benedict-style dish?

Serves 4

50g butter
250g fresh spinach leaves
4 free-range eggs
120ml (8 tablespoons) whipping cream
¼ teaspoon freshly grated nutmeg
crushed sea salt and freshly ground black pepper

Preheat the oven to 180°C/350°C/gas mark 4. Heat the butter in a non-stick frying pan. Add the spinach and sauté for 3 minutes until the spinach is just wilted. Season with crushed sea salt and freshly ground black pepper. Turn out onto a chopping board and chop finely. Divide the spinach between four ramekin dishes.

Make a small well in the centre of the spinach and carefully crack the eggs into the wells. Pour 2 tablespoons of cream over each egg and top with a little freshly grated nutmeg.

Bake in the oven for 10–12 minutes, until golden and bubbling. Remove from the oven and leave to stand for 2 minutes. Serve in the ramekins.

EGGS BENEDICT

When I worked in America I found this dish was extremely popular for brunch. Use free-range eggs, good-quality ham, butter and English muffins to really appreciate this all-time global classic.

Serves 4 (Makes 8 halves)

for the hollandaise

2 tablespoons white wine vinegar

5 peppercorns

250g unsalted butter, melted and skimmed

3 large free-range egg yolks

crushed sea salt and freshly ground black pepper

to serve

2 tablespoons white wine vinegar

8 free-range eggs

8 slices smoked ham

2 English muffins, split

For the hollandaise, pour the vinegar into a saucepan and add the peppercorns. Bring to the boil and simmer for 2 minutes until reduced by half. Remove from the heat, strain and set aside.

In a small saucepan warm the melted, skimmed butter. Remove from the heat and set aside.

Place a heatproof mixing bowl over a large pan of simmering water. The base of the bowl should not be in contact with the water. Add the egg yolks and reduced vinegar and whisk together with a balloon or electric hand whisk.

Whisk vigorously until the mixture forms a foam, ensuring it doesn't get too hot. (To prevent the sauce from overheating, take it on and off the heat while you whisk, and scrape the sides with a plastic spatula).

Whisk in a small ladleful of the warmed butter. Repeat until all the butter is incorporated and you have a texture as thick as mayonnaise. Finally, whisk in crushed sea salt and feshly ground black pepper to taste. Remove from the heat and set aside over the pan of hot water.

Bring a large saucepan of water to the boil. Add 2 tablespoons of white wine vinegar. Bring back to the boil and swirl the vinegared water. Poach the eggs by cracking them individually into cups and dropping them into the pan of swirling simmering water. Simmer for 2–3 minutes. Remove with a slotted spoon and drain on kitchen paper.

Toast the muffins and put the halves on warmed serving plates. Place a spoonful of hollandaise on each muffin half. Arrange a piece of ham on top, then top with a poached egg. Spoon over the remaining hollandaise and season with freshly ground black pepper.

POACHED DUCK EGG, ASPARAGUS, MUSHROOM & BACON SALAD

This brunch-style dish is always a winner in my house. Remember to buy local asparagus when in season to get the best flavour, and don't overcook the duck egg!

Serves 4

100g asparagus spears,
  snapped where they break
  naturally to remove woody ends
1 tablespoon olive oil
100g smoked lardons
150g mushrooms (preferably
  chestnut), wiped and halved
4 duck eggs
crushed sea salt and freshly
  ground black pepper
50g (handful) watercress,
  washed and
  destalked

Preheat the oven to 220°C/425°F/gas mark 7. Place the asparagus spears in a single layer on a small roasting tin. Drizzle with olive oil and sprinkle with salt. Roast for 8 minutes. Remove from the oven and set aside.

In a small non-stick pan, fry the lardons for 4 minutes over a high heat until golden. Remove from the pan with a slotted spoon, drain on kitchen paper and keep warm. Return the pan to the heat and add the mushrooms. Fry in the fat from the lardons for 4 minutes. Add a teaspoon of olive oil to the pan if there isn't enough fat from the lardons. Remove from the heat and set aside.

Poach the duck eggs by cracking them individually into cups and dropping them into a pan of simmering water. Simmer for 4 minutes. Remove with a slotted spoon and drain on kitchen paper.

Arrange the asparagus spears on serving plates, top with the poached eggs. Season with freshly ground black pepper. Scatter over the lardons, mushrooms and watercress leaves. Drizzle over any remaining juices from the frying pan.

SCRAMBLED DUCK EGG WITH SMOKED SALMON & CHIVES

Creamy, rich and velvety. Pick up duck eggs from your local farm shop or supermarket and team with top-quality smoked salmon... sorted!

Serves 4

4 duck eggs

150ml double cream

25g butter

1 tablespoon fresh chives, finely chopped

200g smoked salmon (preferably scottish or dartmouth)

pinch of crushed sea salt and freshly ground black pepper

Whisk the eggs, cream and salt together until combined and the mixture formed is of uniform consistency.

Heat a large non-stick frying pan over a medium heat for 1 minute. Add the butter and let it melt – don't allow it to burn. Pour in the egg mixture and let it sit for 20 seconds without stirring. Stir with a wooden spoon, lifting and folding it over from the bottom of the pan. Let it sit over the heat for another 10 seconds then stir and fold again.

Repeat until the eggs are softly set and slightly runny in places, then remove from the heat and fold the chives through.

Arrange the smoked salmon on serving plates. Season with freshly ground black pepper. Spoon over the scrambled egg.

MACKEREL & CRÈME FRAÎCHE POTATO SALAD

Really fresh mackerel is a must and new potatoes add great taste. I use crème fraîche in the salad because it works well with the oily rich mackerel. Serve with lemon wedges for your naughty sixth ingredient!

Serves 4

350g new potatoes,
 particularly Anja potatoes,
 peeled and cut into 1cm dice
2 tablespoons crème fraîche
2 shallots, finely chopped
1 tablespoon fresh chives,
 finely chopped
1 tablespoon olive oil
4 mackerel fillets, pin-boned
crushed sea salt and freshly
 ground black pepper

Bring a large saucepan of salted water to the boil. Add the potatoes and boil rapidly over a high heat for 3 minutes. Remove from the heat and drain well. Return the potatoes to the pan. Fold in the crème fraîche, shallots and chives. Season with crushed sea salt and freshly ground black pepper.

Heat the olive oil in a non-stick frying pan. Season the mackerel fillets with crushed sea salt and freshly ground black pepper. Add the mackerel, skin-side down, to the pan and cook over a medium heat for 3 minutes. Turn and cook for a further 2 minutes. Remove from the heat.

Arrange the seared mackerel fillets on warmed serving plates. Spoon over the potato salad and drizzle with any remaining juices.

MUM'S ROAST RED PEPPERS & ANCHOVIES

This recipe is from my Mum who is a great home cook. She cooks this dish for Dad in summer and he loves it. Try it for yourselves – either hot or cold.

Serves 4

1 x 50g tin anchovies in oil
4 red peppers
16 cherry tomatoes, halved
3 **garlic** cloves, peeled and thinly sliced
2 sprigs fresh rosemary (leaves picked from the stems and chopped)
crushed sea salt and freshly ground black pepper

Preheat the oven to 200°C/400°F/gas mark 6. Drain the anchovies in a sieve, reserving the oil. Cut the peppers in half lengthways, right through the stalks, and remove the seeds. Brush the peppers with the anchovy oil and place on a baking sheet. Season with crushed sea salt (not too much as the anchovies are very salty) and freshly ground black pepper and roast for 20 minutes, until just tender. Remove from the oven.

Place the cherry tomatoes in a bowl with the sliced garlic and rosemary leaves and toss together. Spoon into the pepper halves. Arrange the anchovy fillets in a criss-cross pattern over the filling and drizzle over any remaining anchovy oil.

Bake for 15–20 minutes until softened and serve warm, or chill and serve as an antipasti.

SALMON WITH CARAMEL CROÛTONS & CONFIT OF LEMON & ROCKET

I love this dish: the warm salmon, crisp sweet croûtons and tangy lemon work so well together. If you don't fancy salmon you can try the recipe with fresh, sustainably-caught tuna.

Serves 4

for the confit of lemon
2 lemons, peeled
50ml water
100g caster sugar

for the caramel croûtons
2 x 2.5cm slices white bread, from an unsliced loaf
150g caster sugar
1 tablespoon olive oil

400g organic salmon fillet, skin on and scaled
25g (handful) rocket leaves
crushed sea salt and freshly ground black pepper

For the confit of lemon, use a small paring knife to cut between the thin skin (membrane) of the lemon to release the segments. Remove any pips before placing the segments in a bowl. Pour the water into a saucepan, add the sugar and bring to the boil, stirring until the sugar has dissolved. Pour over the lemon segments and leave to cool.

For the caramel croûtons, slice the crusts off the bread and discard. Cut the bread into 2.5cm cubes. Place the sugar in a pan and heat over a low heat until the sugar begins to dissolve. Watch it carefully and when it begins to melt, swirl the pan to ensure an even colour (do not stir the sugar).

Once it is an even golden colour, remove from the heat and toss the bread into the pan. Stir to coat. Using a slotted spoon, remove the caramel croûtons from the pan and transfer onto a sheet of baking parchment to cool.

Heat the oil in a large non-stick frying pan over a high heat. Season the salmon with crushed sea salt and freshly ground black pepper. Cut the fillet in half and then divide each piece in half again. Place the salmon fillets in the hot pan, skin-side down, and cook for 4 minutes. Turn and cook for a further minute.

Arrange the fish on warmed serving plates, with the rocket, caramel croûtons and confit of lemon slices.

HONEY, LIME & SOY KING PRAWNS WITH PAK CHOI

The biggest juiciest prawns I have ever eaten were in the Far East. This recipe is my idea of the perfect holiday food!

Serves 4

16 large raw king prawns, peeled and deveined

1 tablespoon dark soy sauce

2 tablespoons blossom honey

zest and juice of 1 lime

2 teaspoons olive oil

100g (2) baby pak choi, sliced

Rinse the prawns and pat dry on kitchen paper. Pour the soy sauce into a small saucepan. Add the honey, lime zest and juice. Bring to the boil, reduce the heat and simmer over a low heat for 4–5 minutes until reduced by half and syrupy. Remove from the heat and set aside.

Heat a large wok or non-stick frying pan over a high heat for 1 minute. Add the olive oil. Heat for 30 seconds. Add the prawns and stir-fry over a high heat for 15 seconds. Add the soy sauce syrup and stir-fry for a further 15 seconds. Add the pak choi and stir-fry for 10–20 seconds until the leaves are just wilted (don't overcook the pak choi as its water content will make the sauce too runny). Serve immediately.

SALT & CHILLI SQUID

Make sure you use seriously fresh squid. The secret here is to use a good thick-bottomed non-stick frying pan taken to a high heat to cook the squid really quickly. The salt and chilli add a kick to the soft squid but be careful not to overcook it, otherwise it can be like rubber. Serve with lemon wedges and sweet chilli sauce for that perfect combination.

Serves 4

500g squid, cleaned

2 tablespoons cornflour

2 tablespoons plain flour

1½ tablespoons hot chilli powder

1 tablespoon szechuan peppercorns, dry roasted and crushed

2 tablespoons crushed sea salt

700ml oil, for deep frying

Rinse the squid thoroughly and dry on kitchen paper. Slice horizontally into 1cm rings and set aside.

Place the cornflour in a mixing bowl with the plain flour, chilli powder, crushed peppercorns and crushed sea salt. Add the squid and toss in the flour mixture.

Half fill a wok or saucepan with oil and heat to 180°C, or until a cube of bread dropped in turns golden in 30 seconds.

Remove the squid from the flour mixture and shake off any excess flour. Plunge half the squid into the hot oil and cook for 45 seconds. Remove from the oil with a slotted spoon and drain on kitchen paper. Repeat with the remaining squid.

MUSSELS WITH BASIL & CHILLI

This is cheap and quick to cook and has so much flavour. The rule is if the raw mussels don't close when tapped, don't use them, and if they don't open when cooked, don't eat them!

Serves 4

2kg mussels, **cleaned and beards removed**

1 tablespoon olive oil

3 red chillies **(bird's eye), finely chopped**

100ml dry white wine

150ml whipping cream

25g **(large handful)** fresh basil leaves, **torn**

Scrub the mussels in a large bowl of cold water and discard any that don't close after a sharp tap on the sink. Drain and set aside.

Heat the oil in a pan large enough to hold the mussels, add the chilli and cook over a low heat for 2 minutes until soft. Add the mussels and wine. Cover and cook over a high heat for 2 minutes or until the shells have opened. Discard any mussels that have not opened.

Pour in the cream and cook over a low heat for 2 minutes. Add the basil and stir well. Serve in large warm bowls with rustic bread (see page 162) to mop up the sauce.

TIP
Thai basil would work wonderfully in this dish, so if you can find it, try it!

SCALLOPS WITH CHORIZO, ROCKET & DILL

Scallops and chorizo are the biggest-selling starter we've ever had at our brasserie. I even had complaints from customers when I took the dish off the menu! Try if you can to buy hand-dived scallops that are as fresh as possible.

Serves 4

100g chorizo sausage

12 hand-dived scallops,
  off the shell, coral removed

1 tablespoon olive oil

4 teaspoons balsamic glaze
  (bought)

25g (handful) rocket leaves,
  washed

8 sprigs of fresh dill

crushed sea salt and freshly
  ground black pepper

Preheat the grill to high. Slice the chorizo into 12 slices, no more than 0.5cm thick. Grill for 3 minutes, turning once, until crisp. Remove from the heat, cover with foil and set aside.

Season the scallops with crushed sea salt and freshly ground black pepper. Heat the oil in a wide, heavy-based frying pan and fry the scallops over a high heat for 40 seconds, turn and cook for a further 40 seconds. Remove from the heat.

Arrange the scallops and chorizo on four serving plates. Drizzle over the balsamic glaze and spoon over the warm juices from the grill pan. Sprinkle over the rocket leaves and ga~ with dill.

CRAB LINGUINE WITH BASIL, LEMON & CHILLI

Crab is an old favourite of mine. This dish has such fresh clean flavours, and is best eaten with fresh crusty bread and a glass of chilled white wine.

Serves 4

100ml olive oil
zest and juice of 1½ lemons
4 red chillies (bird's eye), finely chopped
350g fresh linguine
240g white crab meat
25g (large handful) fresh basil leaves, torn
crushed sea salt and freshly ground black pepper

Put the olive oil, lemon zest and chopped chillies into a small pan and place over a gentle heat until they begin to sizzle. Remove from the heat and set aside.

Bring a large saucepan of salted water to the boil. Add the linguine and cook according to the packet instructions (about 7 minutes). Drain well, rinse with boiling water and set aside.

Tip the chilli and lemon oil into the pan that the linguine was cooked in. Add the lemon juice and cook over a medium heat until sizzling. Return the linguine and add the crab meat. Toss gently for 1–2 minutes to warm the crab through.

Fold in the basil and season with crushed sea salt and freshly ground black pepper. Spoon into warmed serving bowls.

PRESSED CHICKEN & PARMA HAM TERRINE

A straightforward terrine. Serve with chutney, piccalilli or a tangy onion marmalade. A perfect accompaniment would be my rustic bread (see page 162).

Serves 4

1.4kg organic chicken thighs on the bone

1 tablespoon olive oil, plus extra for brushing

2 tablespoons fresh thyme leaves

4 garlic cloves, peeled and crushed

1 tablespoon blossom honey

10 slices parma ham

crushed sea salt and freshly ground black pepper

Preheat the oven to 190°C/375°F/gas mark 5. Place the chicken thighs in a roasting tin. Drizzle over the oil, 1 tablespoon of the thyme and the garlic. Mix together with your hands, then roast for 25–30 minutes. Remove from the oven and leave until cool enough to handle. Reserve the pan juices.

Pick the meat from the chicken, discarding the skin and bones. Place the chicken meat in a bowl; add the remaining 1 tablespoon of thyme, the honey and any juices from the roasting pan. Season with crushed sea salt and freshly ground black pepper. Mix together and leave to cool.

Line a 450g terrine mould or loaf tin with cling film and brush with oil. Line with slices of parma ham so that they overlap to cover the base and sides and overhang the edges.

Spoon in the chicken mixture then fold over the parma ham to encase the terrine. Fold the cling film over and press down gently. Place unopened packs of butter on the top to weigh it down (or whatever you can find) and chill overnight.

To serve, lift the terrine out of the dish, remove the cling film and carefully slice onto serving plates.

Main Events

Everything from quick mid-week suppers to slow braised dishes and dinner party favourites.

ROAST TURBOT WITH GIROLLES

Turbot is the king of the sea. It is not a cheap fish, but cooked well has brilliant taste and it's so delicate it practically melts in your mouth. Teamed with the unique nutty flavour of girolle mushrooms, this is one of my favourite recipes.

Serves 4

4 x 150g tranches of turbot
(thick fillets trimmed
and boned)
1 tablespoon olive oil, plus extra
for brushing
125g girolles (or other wild
mushrooms)
2 shallots, finely chopped
125ml red wine
125ml good chicken stock
crushed sea salt and freshly
ground black pepper

Preheat the oven to 190°C/350°F/gas mark 5. Season the underside of the turbot fillets with crushed sea salt and freshly ground black pepper and brush both sides with oil. Heat an ovenproof frying pan over a high heat and sear the turbot for 30 seconds on each side. Transfer the pan to the oven and bake for 8 minutes.

Meanwhile, heat the oil in a non-stick frying pan and fry the girolles for 5 minutes. Remove from the pan with a slotted spoon and set aside.

Return the pan to the heat and add the shallots. Cook over a low heat for 4 minutes until soft. Add the red wine to the pan. Bring to the boil then simmer until reduced by half. Add the chicken stock and bring back to a simmer. Season with crushed sea salt and freshly ground black pepper.

Arrange the turbot on warmed serving plates. Spoon over the girolles and drizzle the sauce around the fish.

JOHN DORY WITH BEURRE BLANC

The john dory or st pierre, is a flavoursome, sweet-tasting fish that is teamed with a rich classic butter sauce in this recipe. Always use unsalted butter for the sauce as salted will be far too strong. For a cheaper but great alternative to john dory use fillets of hake or pollock.

Serves 4

125g cold unsalted butter, diced
2 shallots, finely chopped
75ml dry white wine
1 tablespoon white wine vinegar
1 tablespoon olive oil
8 john dory fillets, skinned
crushed sea salt and freshly ground black pepper

Melt 25g of the butter in a small non-stick pan. Add the shallots and cook over a low heat for 4 minutes until soft. Add the wine and vinegar. Increase the heat and simmer until reduced to about 1 tablespoon (practically nothing).

Whisk the remaining 100g of cold butter into the reduction one cube at a time, whisking continuously. The sauce will emulsify and resemble a loose custard. Season with crushed sea salt and freshly ground black pepper.

Remove from the heat and pass through a fine sieve. Set aside at room temperature and warm gently when ready to serve.

Heat the olive oil in a large non-stick frying pan over a high heat. Season the john dory fillets with crushed sea salt and freshly ground black pepper. Place the fillets in the hot pan, skin- side down and cook for 2 minutes. Turn and cook for a further minute. Remove from the heat.

Arrange the fish on warmed serving plates. Pour over the pan juices and spoon over the butter sauce.

FOIL-WRAPPED BAKED SALMON WITH CHILLI, ORANGE, SOY & SPRING ONION

The inspiration for this recipe came from a holiday in Thailand. Cooked on a barbecue, the dish tastes and smells even better. This method can be used to cook any fish fillets or even whole fish. I have served variations of the dish at our restaurants over the years and it has been extremely popular. Our waiting staff rip open the foil bags at the table and the emerging steam from the dish smells wonderful. I would recommend a portion of fresh egg noodles to accompany this – whatever fish you use.

Serves 4

juice of **6** oranges, **plus the zest of 2**

2 tablespoons dark soy sauce

2 red chillies **(bird's eye), finely chopped**

6 spring onions, **trimmed and sliced**

4 x 100g organic salmon fillets, **skin on**

olive oil for brushing

crushed sea salt and freshly ground black pepper

Pour the orange juice into a bowl with the zest and the soy sauce. Add the chopped chillies and spring onion and stir together.

Lay four double-layer 30-cm squares of foil over four shallow bowls and push down into the bowls. Season the salmon fillets with crushed sea salt and freshly ground black pepper.

Place one salmon fillet in the middle of each square of indented foil. Pour the orange mixture over each piece of salmon. Gather up the corners of each foil square and crimp together to form a rough pyramid shape.

Heat two large non-stick frying pans over a high heat for 1 minute (if you don't have two frying pans, use a deep-based baking tray). Brush the base of the foil pyramids with oil. Place the foil pyramids into the two pans (or baking tray) and cook for 6 minutes until the pyramids are puffed up and you can hear the contents simmering.

Carefully remove from the pan. To serve, rip open the foil pyramids at the table and let the aroma fill the room.

STEAMED SEA BREAM WITH CRUSHED POTATOES

Sea bream fillets are a cheaper alternative to sea bass but have a similar texture and flavour. They are quick to steam and the sweet carrot and pungent wholegrain mustard create a great sauce that marries really well with the fish – or on its own with pasta for a delicious vegetarian meal.

Serves 4

500g new season potatoes, scrubbed but not peeled
75g cold unsalted butter, diced
1 tablespoon olive oil
300ml fresh carrot juice
1 tablespoon wholegrain mustard
4 x 150g sea bream fillets
crushed sea salt and freshly ground black pepper

Cut the potatoes into quarters. Bring a large pan of salted water to the boil and add the potatoes. Bring to the boil and simmer for 12 minutes until just cooked. Drain well, return to the pan and crush with 25g of the butter, the olive oil and crushed sea salt. Cover and set aside. Keep warm.

Pour the carrot juice into a large non-stick frying pan. Bring to the boil, reduce the heat and simmer for 4–5 minutes until reduced by half. Skim off any scum and discard. Stir in the mustard and whisk in the remaining 50g of butter until melted and glossy. Season with crushed sea salt and freshly ground black pepper. Keep warm over a low heat.

Half-fill the base of a steamer with water and bring to the boil. Season the sea bream fillets with crushed sea salt and freshly ground black pepper. Wrap each fillet in cling film. Place in the steamer and steam for 4 minutes until cooked.

Arrange the crushed potatoes on warmed serving plates. Unwrap the sea bream, place on top of the potatoes and spoon the carrot and mustard sauce around the fish.

PLAICE FILLETS WITH PANCETTA & BROWN NUT BUTTER

I love this combination: soft, just-cooked plaice fillets with crispy cured pancetta bacon and rich brown nut butter makes for the perfect meal. Serve with sautéd young leaf spinach and new potatoes for a seriously good supper!

Serves 4

12 thin slices pancetta
2 tablespoons olive oil
100g butter
12 plaice fillets (about 60g each)
juice of 1 lemon
2 tablespoons chopped fresh flat-leaf parsley
crushed sea salt and freshly ground black pepper

Preheat the grill to high. Grill the pancetta for 3 minutes, turning once, until crispy. Remove from the grill and drain on kitchen paper. Preheat the oven to 130°C/275°F/gas mark 1.

Heat the oil and 25g of the butter in a non-stick frying pan. Season the plaice fillets and cook, skin-side up, for 2 minutes. Turn and cook for a further 2 minutes. Remove from the heat, transfer to an ovenproof dish and place in the oven with the pancetta to keep warm.

In a separate non-stick frying pan heat the remaining 75g butter over a medium heat. When the butter starts to smell nutty and turns golden, add the lemon juice and parsley. Bring back to boiling point and remove from the heat. Season with crushed sea salt and freshly ground black pepper.

Arrange the plaice fillets on warmed serving plates. Top with the pancetta and spoon over the brown nut butter.

POACHED LEMON SOLE WITH TOMATOES & TAPENADE

This recipe is a toned-down taste of Provence: delicate lemon sole fillets, rich tomatoes, salty tangy tapenade and fresh basil. It works well served with new potatoes or pasta and, for a more classic touch, add some roast garlic cloves to the sauce before serving.

Serves 4

12 lemon sole fillets, skinned
50g black olive tapenade
1 handful (25g) basil leaves, plus extra for garnish
300ml passata
150ml boiling water
40g french green beans, blanched and sliced on the diagonal
crushed sea salt and freshly ground black pepper

Lay the fillets of sole out flat and spread each one with tapenade paste. Lay the basil leaves over the tapenade and roll up each fillet. Secure the fillet parcels together with cocktail sticks.

Pour the passata and boiling water into a large, deep frying pan and bring to the boil. Reduce the heat, add the fish, cover the pan and poach over a medium heat for 2 minutes. Turn the fish and poach for a further 2 minutes.

Carefully remove the fish and set aside, keeping warm. Add the green beans to the pan, season with crushed sea salt and freshly ground black pepper. Bring to the boil and cook over a high heat for 2 minutes.

Arrange the fish on warmed serving plates. Spoon the sauce around the fish and garnish with torn basil.

BEER BATTERED FISH

This recipe uses vast amounts of fresh yeast that can be purchased from any good bakery or supermarket bakery counter. The finished batter is quite simply amazing and produces the best battered fish ever. Just add chips!

Serves 4

250ml lager
200g plain flour, sifted, plus extra for dusting
½ teaspoon caster sugar
250g fresh yeast
700ml sunflower or other light cooking oil for deep frying
4 x 200g fresh white fish fillets, skinned (hake, coley or line-caught sea bass)
pinch of crushed sea salt

Pour the beer into a mixing bowl. Add the flour, sugar, yeast and salt. Whisk together to make a smooth thick batter. Cover with a damp tea towel and prove at room temperature for 30 minutes.

Half-fill a saucepan or wok with oil and heat to 180°C, or until a cube of bread dropped in turns golden in 30 seconds.

Take a fish fillet by its tail end and dust with flour. Dip in the batter and plunge into the hot oil. Repeat with the remaining 3 fish fillets. Cook for 4 minutes, turning after 2 minutes, until golden. Carefully remove with a slotted spoon and drain on kitchen paper.

Serve with homemade tartare sauce (see page 169).

GUINEA FOWL WITH ONION SOUBISE

A touch of classic French cookery. When you eat it you will understand why the classics are still the best.

Serves 4

15g butter
4 free-range guinea fowl
  breasts
crushed sea salt and freshly
  ground black pepper

For the soubise
25g butter
1 large onion, finely chopped
½ teaspoon fresh thyme
  leaves
150ml whipping cream

Preheat the over to 200°C/400°F/gas mark 6. Melt the butter in a small pan and use to grease a roasting tin and a sheet of parchment paper, cut to the same size as the roasting tin.

Rub the guinea fowl breasts with crushed sea salt and freshly ground black pepper. Place in the roasting tin and cover with the buttered parchment paper. Roast for 20 minutes.

For the soubise, melt the butter in a non-stick saucepan. Add the onions and stir to coat in the butter. Cover and cook over a low heat for 20 minutes, stirring every 5 minutes, until softened but not coloured. Add the cream, bring to the boil and simmer, uncovered, over a low heat until the cream has reduced by half. Add the thyme leaves and season with crushed sea salt and freshly ground black pepper.

Remove the guinea fowl from the oven and leave to rest for 3 minutes. To serve, carve the breast and fan out on warmed serving plates. Spoon over the onion soubise.

GREEN CURRY

Most people I know love a green curry. Here is a quick cheat's way to curry heaven.

Serves 4

1 tablespoon olive oil

2 tablespoons green curry paste

750g free-range, skinless and boneless chicken breast, cut into chunks

zest and juice of 1 lime

400ml coconut milk

15g (small handful) fresh coriander, chopped

Heat the oil in a wok or large frying pan. Add the curry paste and cook over a high heat for 1 minute. Add the chicken, lime zest and coconut milk. Bring to the boil, then reduce the heat and simmer for 15–20 minutes until thickened slightly.

Stir in the chopped coriander and lime juice. Leave to stand for a few minutes to allow the sauce to become creamier before serving. You will taste the true flavours of the curry paste when the sauce is slightly cooler.

STIR-FRIED CHILLI CHICKEN

Pushed for time and want to cook something fresh with a bit of a kick? Then try this! It really is a meal in minutes that tastes fantastic and beats any takeaway hands down. The ultimate quick chilli chicken. Serve with fresh egg noodles or rice.

Serves 4

4 garlic cloves, peeled

2 red chillies (bird's eye), halved

2 tablespoons olive oil

4 skinless, boneless chicken fillets, sliced

1 tablespoon dark soy sauce

25g (large handful) fresh basil leaves, torn

Place the garlic and the chillies in a mortar with 2 teaspoons of the olive oil and grind with the pestle to a paste.

Heat a wok or a large non-stick frying pan over a high heat for 1 minute. Add the remaining olive oil and the garlic-chilli paste. Stir-fry for 10 seconds.

Add the chicken and stir-fry for a further 4 minutes. Add the soy sauce and torn basil and stir-fry for another 1 minute until the basil has wilted. Serve immediately.

THAI ROAST CHICKEN

A roast with a kick! I cook this for my friends when they come over and we watch the Grand Prix on tv. We always argue about who is the best driver and, as an accompaniment to the meal, we always have a crate of ice-cold beer! I usually serve this dish with sesame noodles.

Serves 4

2 red chillies (bird's eye), halved and deseeded

150g creamed coconut

zest and juice of 2 limes, plus 2 limes, sliced

25g (handful) fresh coriander

1.5 kg free-range chicken

Preheat the oven to 190°C/350°F/gas mark 5. Put the chillies and creamed coconut in a food processor with the lime zest, lime juice and coriander. Blend to a smooth paste.

Loosen the skin at the top of the crown of the chicken and push your index and middle fingers underneath to form a pocket. Score the thighs twice on both sides.

Push most of the paste into the pocket under the skin and rub the remaining paste into the thighs of the chicken.

Lay the lime slices on the bottom of a roasting pan and sit the chicken on top. Cover with foil and roast for 40 minutes. Remove from the oven, remove the foil and baste the chicken. Return to the oven, uncovered, and cook for a further 30–40 minutes, basting occasionally. Remove from the oven and rest for 5 minutes.

Carve the chicken onto warmed serving plates.

GINGER & HOI SIN DUCK WITH GLASS NOODLES

A taste of the orient. Go to a local Chinese supermarket for the ginger in syrup and, while you're there, pick up a packet of glass or cellophane noodles to serve this with. Tangy ginger and flavoursome hoi sin work so well with duck. Make sure you render the duck breasts well when cooking to get that ultimate crispy skin.

Serves 4

4 x 6oz boned duck breast
(**Gressingham or Creedy Carver**)

3 pieces of stem ginger
in syrup, **chopped, plus
1 tablespoon of the syrup**

2 tablespoons hoi sin sauce

6 spring onions, **trimmed and chopped**

200g dried glass noodles

Prick the duck skin with a fork. Heat a large non-stick frying pan over a high heat for 2 minutes. Add the duck breasts, skin-side down, and cook over a medium heat for 10 minutes. Spoon off the fat and discard. Turn the duck breast and cook for a further 2 minutes. Remove from the heat, cover and leave to stand.

Return the pan to the heat. Add the chopped ginger and the syrup and cook over a low heat for 1 minute. Increase the heat; add the hoi sin and 2 tablespoons of water. Cook for 1 minute. Add the spring onions and cook, stirring, for 2 minutes until the onions have wilted. Reduce the heat to very low to keep the sauce warm.

Bring a large pan of salted water to the boil and drop in the glass noodles. Cook for 2 minutes, drain well and spoon onto warmed serving plates. Slice the duck breast on the diagonal and arrange over the noodles. Spoon over the ginger and hoi sin sauce.

ROAST DUCK WITH MAPLE & BLACKBERRIES

A twist on a classic recipe. Try this in the blackberry season (end of summer to early autumn) when the berries are at their best.

Serves 4

1 x 1.5kg duck (gressingham or creedy carver)

1 tablespoon olive oil

200g blackberries

2 tablespoons maple syrup

3 tablespoons crème de cassis (blackcurrant liqueur)

300ml good chicken stock

crushed sea salt and freshly ground black pepper

Preheat the oven to 200°C/400°F/gas mark 6. Using a roasting fork or skewer, lightly prick the skin of the duck all over (you don't want to pierce the meat). Place the duck on a wire rack in or over the sink. Bring a kettle of water to the boil and pour the boiling water over the duck. Leave to stand for 2 minutes and pat dry with kitchen paper. Rub the duck with olive oil and crushed sea salt.

Place the duck, breast-side down, on the wire rack set over a heavy-based roasting tin. Roast in the oven for 20 minutes. Remove from the oven and turn the duck, breast-side up. Return to the oven and cook for a further 40 minutes. Remove from the oven, set the duck and the rack aside.

Drain all the fat from the roasting tin (reserve the fat for when you want to roast potatoes). Place the tin over a high heat, add the blackberries, maple syrup, crème de cassis and chicken stock and bring to the boil stirring. Remove from the heat. Return the duck to the pan and sit in the blackberry liquid. Return to the oven and cook for a further 15 minutes.

Place the duck on a warm plate. Cover with foil and leave to rest for 15 minutes before carving. To serve, place the roasting pan over a medium heat to warm the sauce through. Season to taste with crushed sea salt and freshly ground black pepper. Carve the duck and serve with the blackberry sauce.

POT AU FEU

An easy 'all in one pot' method of cooking. Eat this on a cold winter's day. Any remaining broth makes a great soup.

Serves 4

1.5kg (medium) free-range chicken

3 leeks, cut into large chunks

4 carrots, peeled and cut into large chunks

small bunch fresh thyme, tied with string

1.2 litres (2 pints) hot chicken stock

crushed sea salt and freshly ground black pepper

Preheat the oven to 190°C/375°F/gas mark 5. Place the chicken in a large casserole dish. Add the leeks, carrots and thyme. Pour over the chicken stock (there should be enough stock to cover the ingredients).

Cover the casserole dish and put into the oven. Cook for 2 hours. Remove from the oven and discard the bunch of thyme. Season with crushed sea salt and freshly ground black pepper.

Remove the chicken from the casserole and carve the meat – it should fall off the bones. Ladle the vegetables into warmed serving bowls and top with the chicken. Ladle over the stock.

GNOCCHI WITH BACON & PEAS

Gnocchi can be eaten with many things. This is how I love to eat it. Add a few plum tomatoes and a chopped red pepper if you're not a fan of peas.

Serves 4

3 large potatoes (king edward)
1 free-range egg yolk
300g plain flour, sifted
200g smoked bacon lardons
150g garden peas (defrosted from frozen)
crushed sea salt and freshly ground black pepper

Preheat the oven to 180°C/350°F/gas mark 4. Place the potatoes on a baking tray and bake for 1 hour, or until the flesh is fluffy. Cut the potatoes in half, scoop out the flesh and discard the skins.

Pass the potato through a ricer or wire sieve into a large bowl. Add the egg yolk and flour, a little at a time, and mix together until you have a light dough. Cut the dough into six pieces. Use your hands to roll each piece into a long (about 45cm) sausage shape then cut each one into 2cm pieces. Press each piece over the back of a fork.

Heat a heavy-based frying pan. When hot, dry-fry the lardons for 5 minutes until golden. Remove the lardons from the pan with a slotted spoon and drain on kitchen paper. Set the pan aside.

Bring a large saucepan of salted water to the boil. Add the gnocchi and boil for 3–4 minutes, until the gnocchi rise to the surface. Remove from the heat, drain well and set aside.

Return the lardon pan to the heat. Add the gnocchi and toss over a high heat in the fat from the lardons for 3 minutes until golden. Add the defrosted peas and cook for a further 2 minutes. Return the lardons to the pan and season with crushed sea salt and plenty of freshly ground black pepper. Cook for 1 minute to heat through and serve immediately on warmed plates.

CHORIZO PENNE

Chorizo and sherry vinegar work so well together. With a touch of cream and pasta this becomes a quick and simple treat.

Serves 4

350g dried penne
250g chorizo sausage
1 tablespoon olive oil
2 shallots, **finely chopped**
2 tablespoons sherry vinegar
125ml whipping cream

Bring a large saucepan of salted water to the boil. Add the penne and cook according to the packet instructions (about 10 minutes).

Slice the chorizo on the diagonal into thin slices, no thicker than 0.5cm. Heat the oil in a non-stick pan, add the shallots and cook over a medium heat for 2 minutes to soften. Add the chorizo and cook over a high heat for 2 minutes until it begins to release oil. Add the sherry vinegar and cook for 1 minute over a high heat, stirring to deglaze the pan. Add the cream, bring to the boil, stirring, and remove from the heat. Season with crushed sea salt and freshly ground black pepper

Drain the penne. Spoon into warmed serving bowls and pour over the chorizo sauce.

TIPS

If you are cooking for your kids and don't want to use chorizo, cook off some good-quality sausages, slice them and add them before you add the cream.

For a lighter alternative, use half-fat crème fraîche instead of cream.

MUM'S TOAD IN THE HOLE

This reminds me of my childhood. Serve hot, with peas, mashed potato and thick onion gravy, or however your mum used to serve it!

Serves 4

8 great quality sausages
(pork and spiced apple
are good)

1 onion, sliced

2 tablespoons olive oil

crushed sea salt and freshly
ground black pepper

for the batter

100g plain flour

2 free-range eggs

300ml full-fat milk

pinch of crushed sea salt

Preheat the oven to 220°C/425°F/gas mark 7. Put the sausages in a medium roasting tin (so they are quite snug). Scatter over the onion, season with crushed sea salt and freshly ground black pepper and drizzle with the olive oil. Bake in the oven for 10–15 minutes until the sausages are beginning to brown and the onions are tinged at the edges.

For the batter, sift the flour into a mixing bowl with the salt. Make a well in the centre and crack in the eggs. Beat lightly, then gradually pour in the milk, beating all the time, until you have a smooth batter.

Remove the roasting tin from the oven and pour the batter over the sausages. Return to the oven for a further 25–30 minutes until the batter is crisp, golden and well risen. Serve immediately.

GARLIC ROAST PORK FILLET WITH MAPLE-CHILLI ONIONS

Fillets of pork are great on price, low in fat and cook quickly, and the onions add a sweet and sour flavour that works well with the pork. Serve with seasonal vegetables.

Serves 4

2 x 400g pork fillets

4 garlic cloves, peeled and crushed

2 tablespoons olive oil

2 onions, thinly sliced

2 tablespoons maple syrup

1 teaspoon dried chilli flakes

crushed sea salt and freshly ground black pepper

Preheat the oven to 180°C/350°F/gas mark 4. Using the point of a sharp knife, remove the sinew from the pork fillets to prevent them curling during cooking. Season the pork with crushed sea salt and freshly ground black pepper. Rub over the crushed garlic.

Heat 1 tablespoon of the olive oil in a non-stick frying pan. Add the pork and cook for 1 minute on each side. Remove from the heat and transfer to a roasting tin. Roast in the oven for 12–15 minutes until cooked. Remove from the oven. Cover and leave to rest.

Heat the remaining tablespoon of olive oil in a non-stick frying pan, add the onions and cook over a low heat for 10 minutes until soft. Add the maple syrup and chilli flakes and continue cooking for a further 10 minutes until caramelised.

Cut the pork fillets into medallions and arrange on warmed serving plates. Spoon over the maple-chilli onions.

TIP
This dish works just as well with pork or veal chops.

MERGUEZ SAUSAGES, SAUTÉD POTATOES AND RED ONION

These North African sausages are packed full of flavour and I love them with the sweet red onions and crisp and soft sautéd potatoes. I have even eaten this combination stuffed into a baguette after a late night out with friends – mmm pass the ketchup!

Serves 4

8 merguez sausages
3 red onions, cut into wedges
750g potatoes, peeled and thinly sliced
120ml olive oil
250ml red wine (merlot)
2 tablespoons (handful) fresh flat-leaf parsley, chopped
crushed sea salt and freshly ground black pepper

Preheat the oven to 150°C/300°F/gas mark 2. Heat a large non-stick frying pan over a high heat for 1 minute. Add the sausages and cook over a medium heat for 10–15 minutes until browned and cooked through. Remove from the heat and transfer the sausages to an ovenproof dish. Place in the oven to keep warm.

Return the pan to the heat and add the red onions. Cook in the sausage fat (add a little oil if there is not enough fat) for 10 minutes over a low heat until softened. Remove from the heat and set aside.

Bring a large pan of salted water to the boil, add the potatoes and cook for 3 minutes. Drain well and shake out onto a tray lined with kitchen paper. Leave to cool.

Heat the oil in a large non-stick frying pan until hot. Add the potatoes in a single layer, not too tightly packed. (If your pan isn't large enough, use two, or fry the potatoes in batches). Turn the heat to medium-high, so that the potatoes sizzle and cook for 7 minutes. Turn the potatoes 2 or 3 times during cooking but don't move them until they start to brown underneath.

Remove from the pan with a slotted spoon and drain on kitchen paper. Sprinkle with crushed sea salt and transfer to the oven to keep warm.

Return the onion pan to the heat. Add the wine, bring to the boil, reduce the heat and simmer for 7–10 minutes until reduced by half. Stir in the chopped parsley and season with crushed sea salt and freshly ground black pepper.

Arrange the sausages on warmed serving plates with the sautéd potatoes and red onions.

PORK CHOPS WITH BRAMLEY APPLE MASH & ONION CONFIT

For this recipe buy good thick cut pork chops. Perfect with a sweet onion confit.

Serves 4

75g butter

2 tablespoons olive oil

450g onions, thinly sliced

250g (1 large) bramley apple, peeled, cored and chopped

750g potatoes, peeled and cut into chunks

4 pork chops

crushed sea salt and freshly ground black pepper

Melt 25g of the butter and 1 tablespoon of the oil in a heavy-based saucepan over a high heat. When the butter foams, add the onions, stir to coat in the butter and oil. Reduce the heat, cover and cook over a low heat for 20 minutes, shaking the pan from time to time.

Remove the lid from the pan, stir, and increase the heat to medium. Cook for a further 15 minutes, stirring occasionally. Increase the heat to high and cook, stirring constantly, for 10 minutes, until the onions are a deep golden brown. Remove from the heat and keep warm.

Preheat the oven to 200°C/400°F/gas mark 6. Place the apple in an ovenproof casserole, add 1 tablespoon of water, cover and bake in the oven for 15 minutes until just tender. Remove from the oven and set aside.

Meanwhile, bring a large pan of salted water to the boil, add the potatoes and boil for 15–20 minutes until tender. Drain well and mash with the remaining 50g of butter. Season with crushed sea salt and freshly ground black pepper and fold in the cooked apple. Keep warm.

Using a sharp knife, score the skin of the chops (this will help the chops to crisp while cooking) and season with crushed sea salt and freshly ground black pepper. Heat the remaining 1 tablespoon of oil in a large ovenproof frying pan. Add the chops and cook for 1 minute on each side to seal. Transfer the pan to the oven and cook for 8 minutes. Remove from the oven and leave to rest for 2 minutes.

Divide the bramley mash between warmed serving plates, top each portion with a chop and spoon over the onion confit.

HERB & MUSTARD-COATED LAMB RACK

This is one of my all-time favourite dishes. You can buy brioche from your local bakery or supermarket. I recommend cooking this dish with spring lamb for the very best flavour.

Serves 4

2 french-trimmed racks of lamb

1 tablespoon olive oil

2 tablespoons pommery mustard

crushed sea salt and freshly ground black pepper

for the herb crust

25g (1 roll) brioche

2 tablespoons (handful) fresh flat-leaf parsley, chopped

1 tablespoon fresh rosemary leaves, chopped

Using a sharp knife, cut away the thick layer of fat on the outside of each rack of lamb, trimming off the thin sinewy layer of meat underneath (this will leave you with a thick meaty fillet and a fatty layer that lies against the bones). Discard the trimmed fat. Season the racks with crushed sea salt and freshly ground black pepper.

For the herb crust, break the brioche into pieces and place in a food processor and blitz for 30 seconds to reduce it to fine crumbs. Add the parsley and rosemary and blitz for a further 15 seconds. Set aside.

Heat the oil in a large non-stick pan over a high heat. Add the lamb racks and cook for 2 minutes on each side. Remove from the pan and leave to rest for 5 minutes.

Preheat the oven to 240°C/450°F/gas mark 9. Place the racks, skin-side up, on a chopping board and smother with the mustard. Press a generous handful of the herb crust over the racks and transfer to a medium roasting tin. Roast for 10–15 minutes, depending on how rare you like your lamb. Cover the bones with foil if browning too quickly.

Remove from the oven, cover and leave to rest for 5 minutes before slicing and serving.

ROAST LOIN OF LAMB WITH GINGER & SOY

An Asian-inspired lamb dish with a subtle flavour. Remember that the marinade contains soy sauce, which is salty, so easy on the seasoning for this one! I serve this with noodles.

Serves 4

2 x 1.5kg short cut saddle of lamb, **boned and rolled**

1 tablespoon olive oil

125ml teriyaki marinade

1 tablespoon redcurrant jelly

1 tablespoon dry sherry

2.5cm piece fresh root ginger, peeled and grated

crushed sea salt and freshly ground black pepper

Preheat the oven to 200°C/400°F/gas mark 6. Pierce the fat side of the lamb all over with a sharp knife. Season with crushed sea salt and freshly ground black pepper. Rub with olive oil.

Heat a large non-stick frying pan over a high heat for 2 minutes. Sear the lamb for 2 minutes on each side. Remove from the heat and transfer onto a wire rack in a heavy-based roasting tin. Roast in the oven for 15 minutes.

Pour the teriyaki marinade into a bowl. Add the redcurrant jelly, sherry and ginger and stir to a smooth glaze.

Remove the lamb from the oven. Brush half the glaze over the lamb. Return to the oven and roast for a further 10 minutes. Brush again with the remaining glaze and roast for a further 10 minutes. Remove from the oven, cover lightly with foil and leave to rest for 10 minutes before carving.

Carve the lamb onto warmed serving plates and pour over some juices.

6-HOUR BRAISED LAMB SHOULDER

This really is minimum effort for maximum flavour; I wish all cooking could taste this great with so little effort! After the first 30 minutes of cooking turn down the heat and relax – the dish takes care of itself. Serve with potato and celeriac mash and some green beans.

Serves 4

2.2kg blade end shoulder of lamb

1 tablespoon olive oil

12 banana shallots, peeled

10 sprigs fresh thyme, plus 1 tablespoon chopped fresh thyme leaves

24 garlic cloves (about 2 bulbs), peeled

500ml red wine (merlot is good)

crushed sea salt and freshly ground black pepper

Preheat the oven to 200°C/400°F/gas mark 6. Rub the lamb with olive oil and season with crushed sea salt and freshly ground black pepper.

Place the lamb in a heavy-based roasting tin with the shallots and roast for 30 minutes. Remove from the oven and drain off any fat. Add the thyme sprigs and the garlic. Reduce the oven temperature to 130°C/275°F/gas mark 1. Return the lamb to the oven. Cover the tin tightly with foil and cook for 4 ½ hours.

Pour the red wine into a pan and bring to the boil over a medium heat. Remove the roasting tin from the oven and pour the red wine over the lamb. Return the lamb to the oven, covered, and cook for a further hour.

Remove the lamb from the oven and carefully put the lamb, garlic and shallots in a warm serving dish. Be careful as the lamb should be just falling off the bone. Cover and set aside to rest.

Place the roasting tin over a high flame and heat the wine juices. Skim off any fat and stir in the chopped thyme. Season with crushed sea salt and freshly ground black pepper. Pour over the lamb and serve.

SPICED FORE RIB OF BEEF

A spice and meat lover's dream. How thick will you carve your slice?

Serves 4

1 kg piece of free-range fore rib, **on the bone**

4 tablespoons olive oil

2 teaspoons five spice

300g basmati and wild rice

400g purple sprouting broccoli

4 tablespoons black bean sauce

crushed sea salt

Wipe the beef with damp kitchen paper. Pour 1 tablespoon of the oil into a small bowl. Add the five spice and mix together. Rub all over the beef. Cover with cling film and marinate for 4 hours.

Preheat the oven to 200°C/400°F/gas mark 6. Heat 2 tablespoons of the oil in a non-stick pan over a high heat. Add the beef and sear for 30 seconds on all sides. Place the beef in a roasting tin and roast in the oven for 30–35 minutes (for medium rare), basting after 15 minutes.

Remove from the oven and place on a large warm dish. Cover with foil and leave to rest for 15 minutes.

Bring a large pan of salted water to the boil. Add the rice and cook according to the packet instructions. Drain and rinse with boiling water. Return to the pan. Cover with a double layer of kitchen paper and put the pan lid back on. Leave to stand.

Heat the remaining 1 tablespoon of oil in a wok or large or frying pan. Add the broccoli and stir fry for 3 minutes until tender. Add the black bean sauce and stir fry for a further 1 minute.

Carve the beef. Spoon the rice onto warmed serving plates. Arrange the beef and spoon over the stir-fried broccoli.

BANG ON BURGERS

Mix it, cook it, eat it – these burgers are bang on! Serve in floured baps with salad, pickles and your favourite sauce.

Serves 4

2 tablespoons olive oil

I medium onion, finely chopped

650g lean minced beef

1 free-range egg

1 teaspoon paprika (smoked is good)

2 garlic cloves, peeled and crushed

½ teaspoon crushed sea salt and **½ teaspoon** freshly ground black pepper

Heat 1 tablespoon of the olive oil in a non-stick pan and fry the onion over a medium heat for 2 minutes until softened but not coloured. Remove from the heat and set aside to cool.

Break up the mince and place in a bowl. Add the egg, paprika, cooled onions, garlic, salt and pepper. Mix together with your hands.

Divide the mixture into four and shape each piece into a round ball with your hands. Press down to form a burger shape. Place the burgers on a plate, cover with cling film and chill in the fridge for 10 minutes or until required.

Heat the remaining tablespoon of olive oil in a non-stick pan over a medium heat. Add the burgers and cook for 4 minutes. Turn and cook for a further 4 minutes (for medium rare). Remove from the heat and drain on kitchen paper.

BEEF BRAISED IN RED WINE

Slow-braised beef should fall apart as you eat it. This recipe works really well with creamy polenta or more traditionally with herb dumplings.

Serves 4

25g plain flour
700g stewing steak, cubed
3 tablespoons olive oil
2 large onions, cut into wedges
350ml red wine (merlot)
300ml good beef stock
crushed sea salt and freshly
   ground black pepper

Tip the flour into a mixing bowl and season with crushed sea salt and freshly ground black pepper. Add the steak and toss in the flour to coat.

Heat the olive oil in a casserole pan over a high heat. Add the onion wedges and fry for 3 minutes, until just starting to colour.

Tip the beef into the pan and continue frying until browned. Keep the heat high and stir regularly to prevent scorching.

Add the red wine. Bring to the boil, lower the heat and simmer for 4 minutes until the wine has reduced by half.

Pour over the stock. Bring to the boil, reduce the heat, cover and simmer gently for 1 to 1½ hours, until the meat is tender. Season to taste with crushed sea salt and freshly ground black pepper. Ladle into warmed serving bowls.

BEEF FILLET BÉARNAISE

Beef béarnaise is one of my favourites. Buy mature, well-hung marbled beef and rest it well after cooking to produce a truly melt in-the-mouth steak.

Serves 4

for the béarnaise

2 tablespoons white wine vinegar

5 peppercorns, crushed

2 fresh tarragon sprigs, plus 1 tablespoon chopped fresh tarragon leaves

3 large free-range egg yolks

250g unsalted butter, melted and skimmed

crushed sea salt and freshly ground black pepper

for the steak

15g unsalted butter

1 tablespoon olive oil

4 x 175g beef fillets (preferably devon red)

crushed sea salt

For the béarnaise, pour the vinegar into a saucepan, add the peppercorns and tarragon sprigs. Bring to the boil and simmer for 2 minutes until reduced by half. Remove from the heat, strain and set aside.

Warm the melted butter in a small saucepan. Remove from the heat and set aside.

Place a heatproof mixing bowl over a large pan of simmering water. The base of the bowl should not be in contact with the water. Add the egg yolks and reduced wine vinegar and whisk together with a balloon or electric hand whisk. Whisk vigorously until the mixture forms a foam, ensuring it doesn't get too hot. (To prevent the sauce from overheating, take it on and off the heat while you whisk, scraping around the sides with a plastic spatula).

Whisk in a small ladleful of warmed butter. (Go slowly, so that the sauce base doesn't split, or curdle. If it does split, whisk in a teaspoon of boiling water to bring the sauce base back together.) Repeat until all the butter is incorporated and the sauce has a texture as thick as mayonnaise. Finally, whisk in crushed sea salt and freshly ground black pepper to taste. Stir in the chopped tarragon. Remove from the heat and set over the pan of hot water to keep warm.

To cook the steak, melt the butter and oil in a large non-stick frying pan over a medium heat. Season the steak with crushed sea salt, add to the hot pan and brown on both sides. Cook to the desired stage: 2–3 minutes on each side for rare, 3–4 minutes on each side for medium, 5–6 minutes on each side for well done. Remove from the pan and leave to rest for 5 minutes, keeping warm.

Arrange the fillets on warmed serving plates and spoon over the béarnaise.

Vegetable Delights

Quick, big flavoured vegetable dishes for all taste buds! Vegetarians should substitute the cheese in some recipes for the pure rennet-free variety.

POTATO GRATIN

A classic that is great on its own, with a green salad, or can be served as an accompaniment to most meat dishes.

Serves 4

750g potatoes (maris piper or king edward)
300ml whipping cream
1 whole garlic bulb
small bunch fresh thyme, tied
100g gruyère, grated
crushed sea salt and freshly ground black pepper

Peel the potatoes and, using a mandolin or very sharp knife, slice the potatoes very thinly. Cut the garlic bulb in half horizontally.

Pour the cream into a large non-stick frying pan. Add the garlic and thyme. Warm the cream over a low heat. Add the potatoes, bring to the boil, reduce the heat and simmer, over a low heat, uncovered for 15–20 minutes, until the potatoes are soft but still have a little bite.

Preheat the grill to high. Remove the halved garlic bulb and the thyme from the pan. Season well with crushed sea salt and freshly ground black pepper. Pour the cream and potatoes into a 24-cm square gratin dish. Sprinkle over the grated gruyère and grill under a high heat for 2–3 minutes until the gruyère is melted, golden and bubbling. Leave to stand for 2 minutes before serving.

TIP
If you're not a vegetarian, you could add cooked smoked bacon lardons to the gratin before you grill it.

BASIL CRUSHED POTATO CAKE

A simple crispy potato cake with pungent basil. It's brilliant served with crème fraîche. Why not add roast asparagus when it's in season?

Serves 4

750g new potatoes, scrubbed and cut in half

2 tablespoons olive oil

2 shallots, finely chopped

1 garlic clove, peeled and crushed

25g (handful) fresh basil leaves, torn

150ml crème fraîche

crushed sea salt

Bring a large pan of salted water to the boil. Add the potatoes and cook for 15 minutes until just tender. Drain the potatoes and plunge into a bowl of cold water to halt the cooking process. Drain and set aside.

Heat 1 tablespoon of the oil in a non-stick pan. Add the shallots and fry for 2 minutes until soft. Add the garlic and fry for a further minute. Remove from the heat.

Return the potatoes to the pan. Add the shallots and garlic and use the back of a fork to crush each potato against the side of the pan, until it just bursts open. Fold in the basil and crème fraiche.

Divide the mixture between four 9 x 4cm metal chef's rings. Heat the remaining 1 tablespoon of oil in a non-stick frying pan. Add the potato rings and cook over a medium heat for 5 minutes. Turn and cook for a further 5 minutes. Remove the metal rings and serve on warm plates.

PATATAS BRAVAS

This dish is a taste of one of the many tapas plates I enjoyed in Barcelona, whilst drinking chilled beer and staying up late with my friends.

Serves 4

750g floury potatoes (maris piper, desirée or king edward)

100ml olive oil, plus 4 tablespoons

6 ripe tomatoes, deseeded and chopped

3 red bird's eye chillies, finely chopped

crushed sea salt

2 teaspoons black sesame seeds

Preheat the oven to 220°C/425°F/gas mark 7. Peel the potatoes and cut into 2.5cm dice.

Heat 2 tablespoons of the olive oil in large heavy-based roasting tin. Add the potatoes and shake them in the hot oil until covered. Place in the oven and cook for 20–25 minutes until golden brown. Remove from the oven and drain on kitchen paper. Keep warm.

Heat 2 tablespoons of olive oil in a non-stick pan. Add the chopped tomatoes and chilli and cook over a low heat for 10 minutes until the oil begins to separate from the tomatoes. Remove from the heat, pass through a fine sieve and set aside to cool.

Transfer the mixture to the bowl of a food processor and with the motor running, add the 100ml oil in a slow steady stream, until you have a glossy texture that resembles mayonnaise. Season with crushed sea salt.

Tip the hot potatoes into a serving dish and spoon over the tomato chilli sauce. Sprinkle over the black sesame seeds.

BROAD BEAN, MINT & PECORINO SALAD

Fresh sweet broad beans and salty pecorino – great to nibble on a warm summer's night.

Serves 4

1.6kg broad beans in their pods
   or 500g frozen broad beans

zest and juice of 1 lemon

25g (small bunch) fresh mint
   leaves, chopped

100g pecorino (50g grated and
   50g shaved using a peeler)

50ml extra virgin olive oil

50g (large handful) rocket

crushed sea salt and freshly
   ground black pepper

Pod the broad beans if using fresh. Bring a large pan of salted water to the boil, add the beans and cook for 3–5 minutes until tender but still have bite. Drain, refresh in cold water, and peel off the grey skins.

Place the beans in a bowl. Add the lemon zest and juice, chopped mint, the grated pecorino and olive oil. Stir together and season with crushed sea salt and freshly ground black pepper.

Place the rocket in a salad bowl and spoon over the dressed beans. Sprinkle over the pecorino shavings and drizzle over a little olive oil to serve.

SWEET & SOUR LEEKS WITH RICOTTA

It is what it says: sweet and sour. The slightly salty creamy ricotta goes really well with the leeks and makes this dish a winner.

Serves 4

2 tablespoons white wine vinegar

2 tablespoons caster sugar

450ml water

8 baby leeks

1 teaspoon dried chilli flakes

175g ricotta, crumbled

Pour the white wine vinegar into a large pan (large enough to accommodate the leeks whole) and add the sugar and water. Bring to the boil and add the leeks. Bring back to the boil. Reduce the heat, cover and simmer for 8 minutes until the leeks are soft and tender. Remove from the pan and drain, discarding the liquid.

Preheat the grill to high. Using a sharp knife, cut the leeks in half lengthways and place in a 24cm square gratin dish. Sprinkle over the chilli flakes and ricotta. Grill for 3–5 minutes until the ricotta is golden and bubbling.

Leave to stand for 2 minutes before serving.

TIP

If you're not vegetarian, this is a great side dish to serve with a glazed ham hock as it works beautifully with the flavours.

BUTTER BEAN SALAD

So simple to make and it tastes just great. The freshness of the mint with a chilli kick will get your taste buds going!

Serves 4

225g dried butter beans, soaked overnight, or 2 x 397g cans butter beans, drained

juice of 1 large lemon

3 tablespoons olive oil

3 red chillies, (bird's eye) deseeded and finely chopped

1 small red onion, finely chopped

20 fresh mint leaves, torn

crushed sea salt and ground black pepper

If using soaked dried beans, drain and rinse well. Bring a large saucepan of water to the boil. Add the beans, bring to the boil and boil for 10 minutes. Reduce the heat and simmer for 25–30 minutes until soft. Remove from the heat, drain well and leave to cool.

Place the cooled cooked butter beans or drained canned butter beans in a bowl and toss with the lemon juice and olive oil. Add the chopped chilli and red onion. Season to taste with crushed sea salt and ground black pepper. Toss gently to mix. Just before serving add the torn mint leaves.

BUTTERNUT SQUASH & PAK CHOI CURRY

This curry has serious flavour from the spices and sweet butternut squash. Why not experiment with different squashes in the autumn months? Serve with your favourite type of rice and use normal basil if you can't get hold of thai basil.

Serves 4

400ml coconut milk

2 tablespoons yellow curry paste

2kg butternut squash, peeled and cut into chunks

4 baby pak choi, cut into quarters

15g (large handful) fresh thai basil leaves

crushed sea salt

Skim the thick creamy milk from the top of the coconut milk and put it a large non-stick saucepan. Bring the pan to the boil over a high heat and add the curry paste. Cook for 2 minutes, stirring until the coconut and curry paste are combined and sizzling.

Add the remaining coconut milk to the pan with the butternut squash. Bring to the boil, cover and simmer over a low heat for 15 minutes until the squash is tender but not soft. Season to taste with crushed sea salt.

Add the pak choi and simmer for 4 minutes until just wilted. Remove from the heat and stir in the thai basil. Spoon into warmed bowls.

PEPPER POCKETS

I made these once for a veggie friend and they have remained a hit as everyone seems to love them – particularly as part of a picnic, as the pockets transport well.

Serves 4

for the tortillas

200g self-raising flour, sifted

pinch of crushed sea salt

120ml boiling water

1 teaspoon olive oil, plus extra for brushing

for the filling

2 red peppers

1 tablespoon olive oil

200g (1 bag) fresh spinach, chopped

250g emmental, cut into 1cm cubes

75g black niçoise olives, pitted and chopped

freshly ground black pepper

Preheat the oven to 220°C/425°F/gas mark 7. Place the whole peppers on a roasting tray and roast for 25–30 minutes until the skins are starting to blacken. Remove from the oven, place in a freezer bag, seal and set aside for 5 minutes (this helps to loosen their skins). Reduce the oven temperature to 180°C/350°F/gas mark 4.

For the tortillas, sift the flour into a mixing bowl with a pinch of crushed sea salt. Add the water and 1 teaspoon olive oil and mix with your hands to form a soft dough.

Knead for 2 minutes on a lightly floured surface until smooth and elastic. Brush the top of the dough with olive oil, return to the bowl, cover with a clean tea towel and leave to rest for 10 minutes.

For the filling, heat the tablespoon of olive oil in a wok or large non-stick frying pan. Add the spinach and stir fry over a medium heat for 4 minutes until wilted. Remove from the heat and drain in a sieve, squeezing out any excess moisture.

Remove the peppers from the freezer bag. Skin, deseed and slice. Set aside.

Divide the dough into 8 pieces and roll into small balls in your hands. On a lightly floured surface roll each dough ball into a circle roughly 22cm across. Repeat with the remaining dough to make 8 flour tortillas.

Place the spinach in a large bowl. Add the sliced red pepper, emmental and olives. Mix together and season with freshly ground black pepper. Divide the spinach mixture into 8 and spoon into the centre of the 8 tortillas. Brush the edge of each tortilla with water and fold the edges up around the spinach filling to make a parcel.

Heat a large griddle pan over a high heat. Add the tortilla pockets and dry fry for 2 minutes on each side. Transfer to a roasting tin and bake for 12–15 minutes until golden.

Remove from the oven and leave to stand for 2 minutes before serving or leave to cool completely if packing for a picnic.

FIG & MOZZARELLA TART

People use the term 'marriage made in heaven', and this recipe is just that! Add a drizzle of blossom honey or maple syrup if you wish to sweeten things up, or if you're feeling really luxurious, a drizzle of truffle honey. You could serve this with fresh, undressed wild rocket for an added peppery flavour.

Serves 4–6

375g packet shortcrust pastry
2 large free-range eggs
225g mozzarella, **pushed through a grater (don't worry if it crumbles)**
225g ricotta
5 fresh figs, **cut into quarters**
crushed sea salt and finely ground black pepper

Preheat the oven to 200°C/400°F/gas mark 6. Roll out the pastry and line a 20cm diameter (and ideally 5cm deep) loose-based tart tin. Line the pastry with a sheet of baking parchment and fill with baking beans. Bake blind for 20 minutes. Remove from the oven and take out the baking parchment and beans. Reduce the oven temperature to 180°C/350°F/gas mark 4.

Beat the eggs in a mixing bowl. Add the mozzarella and ricotta and mix to a smooth creamy consistency. Season with crushed sea salt and freshly ground black pepper.

Pour the mixture into the baked pastry case or shell. Smooth the surface with a palette knife. Bake for 30 minutes. Remove from the oven and arrange the figs, cut-side up, on the surface. Return to the oven and cook for a further 10 minutes until the figs are beginning to brown on the edges.

Remove from the oven and leave to cool on a wire rack. To serve, remove the tart from the tin and cut into slices. Serve at room temperature.

ASPARAGUS & MINT FRITTATA

Make this frittata when asparagus is in season; it tastes amazing. The mint adds a fresh kick.

Serves 4

225g asparagus
6 free-range eggs
50g parmesan, grated
15g (small bunch) fresh mint
  leaves, picked from the stalks
  and torn
1 tablespoon olive oil
crushed sea salt and freshly
  ground black pepper

Preheat the oven to 200°C/400°F/gas mark 6. Remove the woody ends of the asparagus by bending them and snapping where they break naturally. Bring a large pan of salted water to the boil. Add the asparagus, return to the boil and cook for 3–5 minutes until just tender. Drain and season with crushed sea salt and freshly ground black pepper. Set aside.

Break the eggs into a bowl and beat lightly. Add 40g of the parmesan and the torn mint; season with crushed sea salt and freshly ground black pepper.

Heat the oil in a 20-cm ovenproof frying pan. Add the egg mixture and cook over a low heat, loosening the egg from the sides until it is just starting to set (it should be quite runny).

Arrange the asparagus on the top, sprinkle with the remaining parmesan and bake in the oven for 1 minute only. Loosen the frittata from the pan with a fish slice and transfer to a warm plate. Cut into wedges to serve.

TIP
When asparagus is out of season, you could use garden peas or sautéd slices of courgette.

COUSCOUS SALAD

I had never cooked couscous before I moved to the USA in the mid-1990s, and at that time they were grain mad. This dish always reminds me of that era but it has a modern-day twist that hits all taste buds. The salad can be made in advance and left for up to 12 hours in the fridge, to allow the flavours to blend.

Serves 4

250g couscous

zest and juice of 1½ lemons

475ml boiling water

150g sun-blushed tomatoes, chopped

100g black niçoise olives, pitted and halved

3 tablespoons extra virgin olive oil

250g halloumi, sliced medium-thin (just under 0.5cm)

crushed sea salt and freshly ground black pepper

Place the couscous in a large bowl. Add the lemon zest and juice. Pour over the boiling water. Stir, cover with a clean tea towel and leave to stand for 5 minutes until the lemon liquid is absorbed.

Using a fork, fluff the couscous grains to separate them. Stir in the sun-blushed tomatoes, olives and olive oil. Season well with crushed sea salt and freshly ground black pepper. Mix gently.

Heat a large non-stick griddle pan for 1 minute over a high heat. Reduce the heat to medium and add the halloumi slices. Dry-fry the halloumi for 2 minutes, turn and cook on the other side for a further 2 minutes until they're golden-brown in parts. Remove from the heat and set aside.

Arrange the halloumi slices over the couscous salad.

BLACK RICE SALAD WITH ROASTED PEPPERS & OLIVES

I use black rice for this recipe as it makes the dish a great alternative to ordinary rice salads. You can find it in Chinese stores or supermarkets.

Serves 4

300g black rice

4 yellow peppers

2 tablespoons olive oil

150g mixed sliced olives in oil (on the deli counter of most supermarkets)

2 tablespoons spiced mango chutney (or plain mango chutney)

1 tablespoon sherry vinegar

crushed sea salt and freshly ground black pepper

Preheat the oven to 220°C/425°F/gas mark 7. Bring a large pan of salted water to the boil. Add the rice and cook according to the packet instructions (about 20 minutes). Drain the rice and rinse with boiling water. Transfer to a mixing bowl and set aside to cool.

Meanwhile, place the whole peppers on a roasting tray and roast for 25–30 minutes until the skins are starting to blacken. Remove from the oven, place in a freezer bag, seal and set aside for 5 minutes (this helps to loosen their skins). When cool enough to handle, remove the peppers from the freezer bag. Skin, deseed and slice.

When the rice has cooled, add the roasted peppers, olive oil, mixed olives including the oil, mango chutney and sherry vinegar. Stir to mix. Season to taste with crushed sea salt and freshly ground black pepper.

SPICED LENTILS

This lentil recipe works particularly well with oily fish but I have included it in the vegetarian section of this book because it tastes great on its own.

Serves 4

350g puy lentils, soaked overnight in water

1 tablespoon olive oil

2 garlic cloves, peeled and crushed

2 tablespoons dark soy sauce

2 tablespoon balsamic vinegar

1 teaspoon worcestershire sauce

crushed sea salt and freshly ground black pepper

Drain the soaked lentils. Bring a large pan of salted water to the boil and add the lentils. Bring to the boil, reduce the heat, cover and simmer for 30 minutes until cooked (the lentils should be soft). Remove from the heat and drain in a fine sieve. Set aside.

Heat the olive oil in a large non-stick pan over a low heat, add the garlic and cook for 1 minute until softened but not coloured. Add the lentils to the pan with the dark soy sauce, balsamic vinegar and worcestershire sauce. Cook, stirring, over a medium heat for 4 minutes.

Season with crushed sea salt and freshly ground black pepper before serving.

TIP

For the purist vegetarian who doesn't eat Worcestershire sauce, keep this quick recipe to 4 main ingredients!

PEARL BARLEY RISOTTO

This is a twist on the classic risotto. Pearl barley has a great texture and is an economical way of cooking for large numbers. You could try this with slow cooked red cabbage.

Serves 4

300g pearl barley
1 litre good vegetable stock
    (Marigold swiss vegetable
    bouillon powder)
3 garlic cloves, peeled and
    crushed
1 tablespoon olive oil
4 shallots, finely chopped
150g parmesan, grated
freshly ground black pepper

Tip the pearl barley into a large saucepan. Cover with water and soak, with the lid on, overnight in the fridge.

Drain the soaked pearl barley and rinse under cold running water. Return to the pan with the vegetable stock and 1 of the crushed garlic cloves. Bring to the boil, reduce the heat and simmer for 15 minutes until tender. Drain in a fine sieve, reserving the stock.

Heat the olive oil in a non-stick frying pan. Add the remaining 2 crushed garlic cloves and the shallots. Cook over a medium heat for 2 minutes until softened but not coloured. Add the pearl barley and stir in the parmesan cheese. Cook, stirring, over a low heat for 3 minutes. The mixture will thicken.

Add 4 tablespoons of the reserved stock to loosen the mixture.

Season to taste with freshly ground black pepper before serving.

MUSHROOM & GORGONZOLA RISOTTO

Creamy strong gorgonzola is great in a risotto whilst the mushrooms add a depth of flavour.

Serves 4

25g dried porcini mushrooms

2 tablespoons olive oil

1 large onion, finely sliced

250g chestnut mushrooms, cleaned and cut into quarters

175g risotto rice (carnaroli, arborio or vialone nano)

150g gorgonzola cheese, crumbled

freshly ground black pepper

Place the porcini mushrooms in a bowl. Pour over 750ml boiling water and leave to soak and soften for 30 minutes. Drain in a fine sieve, reserving the mushroom liquid for stock. Squeeze any excess liquid out of the porcini and chop finely.

Heat the oil in a shallow saucepan or deep frying pan over a medium heat. Add the onion and cook for 5 minutes until softened but not coloured. Add the chestnut mushrooms and stir to coat in the oil. Cover the pan with a lid and cook over a low heat for 20 minutes, shaking the pan occasionally until the mushrooms release their juices.

Increase the heat, add the rice to the pan and stir to coat all the grains in oil. Stir in the chopped porcini. Add a quarter of the reserved mushroom liquid and simmer over a medium heat, stirring until the rice has absorbed the liquid. Add the same amount of stock again and continue to simmer and stir (the rice will start to become plump and tender). Continue adding the stock slowly, stirring constantly until all the liquid has been absorbed (it should take about 20 minutes). If the rice is undercooked and you have run out of liquid add a splash of water to the pan.

Remove from the pan and sprinkle over the gorgonzola. Cover and leave to stand for 2 minutes until the cheese has melted. Season with freshly ground black pepper. Give the risotto a final stir and serve.

TIP

You can use any soft blue cheese for this recipe – choose your favourite.

MACARONI CHEESE

Good old macaroni cheese! Serve it with salad and some crusty baguette.

Serves 4

350g macaroni
40g butter
40g plain flour
600ml full-fat milk
crushed sea salt and freshly
   ground black pepper
250g red leicester, grated

Bring a large pan of salted water to the boil. Add the macaroni. Return to the boil, reduce the heat and simmer for 10 minutes.

Melt the butter in a large saucepan over a medium heat. Add the flour and stir to make a roux. Cook over a low heat for 2 minutes. Gradually whisk in the milk a little at a time, whisking between each addition until you have thick, velvety sauce. Bring the mixture to the boil, reduce the heat, then leave on a low simmer.

Preheat the grill to high. Drain the macaroni well and add it immediately to the sauce. Stir in 150g of the grated red leicester and season with crushed sea salt and freshly ground black pepper.

Pour the mixture into a 24cm square ovenproof dish, top with the remaining 100g grated red leicester. Grill under a high heat for 2–3 minutes until the cheese is bubbling and golden. Leave to stand for 2 minutes before serving.

BRUSCHETTA

Great as a starter or nibbles. Use ripe sweet plum tomatoes for the best flavour. Why not use the ciabatta recipe in the bread section?

Serves 4

4 ripe sweet plum tomatoes
½ small red onion, finely
   chopped
15g (small handful) fresh basil
   leaves, torn
1 tablespoon olive oil, plus extra
   for drizzling
12 slices ciabatta (sundried
   tomato ciabatta, see page 165)
1 garlic clove, peeled
crushed sea salt and freshly
   ground black pepper

Roughly chop the tomatoes and place in a bowl with their juices. Add the onion, basil and olive oil. Season with crushed sea salt and freshly ground black pepper. Toss together and set aside.

Heat a griddle pan over a high heat for 1 minute. Add the ciabatta slices and toast lightly for 30 seconds on each side. Remove from the pan.

Rub the toasted ciabatta with the garlic clove and drizzle with olive oil. Spoon the tomato mixture over the ciabatta and serve.

Final Flings

A collection of my all-time favourite dessert recipes – enjoy!

TARTE TATIN

One of the first desserts I ever made in a professional kitchen, this is still one of my firm favourites. Serve with cream or vanilla ice cream.

Serves 4–6

4 granny smith apples
100g unsalted butter
75g caster sugar
1 vanilla pod
200g packet puff pastry

Preheat the oven to 200°C/400°F/gas mark 6. Take a small paring knife and cut each apple into six wedges. Remove the core and pips.

Melt the butter in a 24cm ovenproof non-stick frying pan. Add the sugar and cook over a medium heat for 3 minutes until the sugar is at the golden caramel stage. Add the prepared apples and coat in the caramel.

Cut the vanilla pod in half lengthways and scrape out the seeds with the tip of a knife. Add the seeds to the apples in the pan. Discard the pod. Cook the apples over a low heat for 2 minutes.

Roll out the puff pastry on a lightly floured surface until the piece is big enough to cut out a circle 24cm in diameter. Prick with a fork and place the pastry on top of the apples. Push the edges of the pastry down around the inside edge of the pan.

Bake in the oven for 15 minutes until golden. Remove from the oven and put a large plate on top of the pan. Quickly tip the pan over to release the tarte onto the plate (take care: the caramel juices are very hot).

TIP

You could use pears, firm peaches or nectarines for this recipe instead of the apples; you could even make a banana one, just steer clear of fruit that is too soft as it will fall apart and go soggy.

LEMON TART

Clean but rich and fresh, this tart is the perfect way to end a meal. In the late summer months, serve with a sauce made with fruits in season – raspberry or blackcurrant.

Serves 4–6

1 x 20cm sweet pastry shell **or**
  1 x **300g packet** sweet pastry
5 free-range eggs, **plus 1 egg white**
150g caster sugar
zest and juice of 5 lemons
200ml whipping cream

If using packet sweet pastry, preheat the oven to 200°C/400°F/gas mark 6. Lightly flour the work surface and roll out the pastry to a 30cm circle, 0.5cm thick. Use to line a deep-sided, 20-cm loose-based tart tin. Line the pastry with a sheet of baking parchment and fill with baking beans. Bake for 20 minutes. Take the tart shell from the oven and remove the parchment paper and beans. Reduce the oven temperature (or if you're using a pastry shell, preheat) to 160°C/325°F/gas mark 3.

Meanwhile, break the eggs into a bowl, add the sugar, lemon zest and juice and whisk to combine. In a separate bowl, whisk the cream until thick and velvety but not fully whisked. Fold the cream into the lemon mixture.

Pour the mixture into the part-baked pastry case or shell and bake for 35–40 minutes or until the filling is set and feels springy in the centre. Leave to cool before serving.

RASPBERRY AND PASSION FRUIT MERINGUE ROULADE

Sweet raspberries, tangy passion fruit and crisp but gooey meringue... enough said!

Serves 4

4 free-range egg whites
200g caster sugar
250ml whipping cream
juice and seeds of 3 passion fruit
200g raspberries

Preheat the oven to 180°C/ 350°F/gas mark 4. Line a swiss roll tin (23 x 30cm) with baking parchment.

Place the eggs whites in a bowl and whisk until stiff. Slowly add the sugar, one tablespoon at a time, whisking between each addition, until stiff and glossy.

Spoon the mixture evenly into the lined tin. Bake for 15 minutes, until crisp on the outside. Remove from the oven and leave to cool completely.

Lay a sheet of baking parchment on a work surface. Turn the meringue out onto it. Peel off the baking parchment and discard. Whip the cream until it forms soft peaks then stir in the passion fruit juice.

Spoon the cream over the meringue. Sprinkle over the raspberries and spoon over the passion fruit seeds. Start at one of the shorter ends and roll the meringue up away from you (as you would a swiss roll), using the baking parchment to help you turn it over.

Cut into slices and arrange on serving plates.

HONEY BAKED FIGS

Sweet and tangy, buy just-ripe figs so they cook perfectly. Traditionally served with yogurt and almonds but this dish is also divine with crème fraîche and pistachios.

Serves 4

8 **fresh,** ripe figs
3 tablespoons blossom honey
½ teaspoon balsamic vinegar
200ml greek yogurt
25g flaked almonds, **toasted**

Preheat the oven to 220°C/425°F/gas mark 7. Lay a large sheet of foil across a roasting tin, allowing enough foil to overlap on all sides of the tin to wrap the figs in a parcel.

Trim the stalks of each fig and cut a cross into the top of each one. Gently squeeze each fig to open it out. Spoon the honey equally over the top of the figs. Wrap the figs in the foil to form a well-sealed parcel and bake for 10–12 minutes.

Unwrap the parcel and transfer the figs onto serving plates. Drizzle with balsamic vinegar. Add a good spoonful of greek yogurt to each fig and sprinkle with toasted almonds. Finally drizzle over the remaining juices and melted honey from the foil parcel.

TIP
You could use peach or nectarine halves for this recipe instead of the figs.

SUMMER PUDDING

A pure taste of the summer. Use slightly stale bread to soak up the juices and serve with whipped or clotted cream... yummy!

Serves 4

1½ gelatine leaves
250g caster sugar
5 tablespoons water
500g raspberries
500g blueberries
10 slices white bread, crusts removed

Soak the gelatine leaves in a little cold water for 4–5 minutes until soft. Place the sugar in a heavy-based saucepan with the water. Heat gently, stirring, until the sugar dissolves. Add the raspberries and blueberries and cook over a low heat for 3 minutes until the juices begin to run. Remove from the heat. Squeeze all the water out of the gelatine leaves and add them to the pan. Stir until the gelatine has dissolved. Set aside.

Cut a circle from one slice of bread to fit the base of a 1.1 litre (2-pint) pudding basin. Line the sides with seven slices of bread overlapping the slices, leaving no spaces. Spoon in the fruit, reserving 3 tablespoons of the syrup.

Top the fruit with the remaining two slices of bread and spoon over the reserved syrup. Cover with a plate that exactly fits inside the basin. Place a weight on top to press down and chill in the fridge overnight.

To serve, turn out onto a plate and slice into wedges.

BLACKBERRY & APPLE CRUMBLE

There is nothing better than sweet but tart fruit with a crumbly top. Serve this with my custard recipe (page 172), of course! For a dinner party, you could serve individual crumbles in small oven-proof containers.

Serves 4

for the filling

1.5kg (2 large) bramley cooking apples, **peeled, cored and cut into chunks**

50g caster sugar

1 tablespoon water

200g blackberries

for the crumbles

150g plain flour

80g cold butter, **cubed**

80g caster sugar

Preheat the oven to 190°C/375°F/gas mark 5. Place the apples in a heavy-based saucepan with the sugar and water. Cook over a low heat for 5 minutes. Add the blackberries, remove from heat and spoon into a shallow 20cm ovenproof dish.

To make the crumble, place the flour in a large bowl and rub in the butter until the mixture resembles fine breadcrumbs. Stir in the sugar.

Sprinkle the crumble mixture over the fruit and bake for 25–30 minutes until the crumble is golden and the apple and blackberries are hot. Serve with custard (see page 172) or ice cream.

TIP

You could add toated oats or crushed hazelnuts for a different crumble experience. And feel free to use varying fruits for your crumble bottom.

CARAMELISED PEACH MILLE-FEUILLE

Crisp puff pastry with warm creamy peaches. Be careful not to overcook the peaches – they should have a slightly firm bite.

Serves 4

375g packet all-butter puff pastry
300g caster sugar
250ml whipping cream
2 ripe peaches, stoned, and each cut into 8 wedges

Preheat the oven to 200°C/400°F/gas mark 6. Roll out the pastry sheet to a 30cm square with 1½cm thickness. Cut the pastry into 4 neat diagonal sheets. Using the point of a small, sharp knife, score the top of your diamonds lightly with a criss-cross effect. Place on a large baking sheet and bake for 15 minutes until golden. Remove from the oven.

Place the caster sugar in a heavy-based pan. Heat over a low heat until the sugar begins to dissolve. Watch it carefully and when it begins to melt, swirl the pan to ensure an even colour, but don't stir. Once it is an even golden colour add 50ml of the cream and the peaches. Stir to coat the peaches in the creamy caramel. Remove from the heat and set aside.

Whisk the remaining 200ml whipping cream until it just holds its shape.

To assemble, slice your pastry diamonds in half lengthways, then put a teaspoon of cream onto the centre of 4 serving plates (to stabilise the pastry) and top with a pastry base at a jaunty angle. Add an eighth of the remaining cream onto the 4 diamond bases, then spoon over 4 peach wedges. Top with the remaining cream. Add a drizzle of the remaining caramel sauce and finish with the diamond lid.

GINGERNUT & MASCARPONE CHEESECAKE

Gingernut biscuits are not just for dunking in your tea!

Serves 4

50g gingernut biscuits
1 vanilla pod, **seeds scraped out, pod discarded**
340g mascarpone
125g caster sugar
250ml whipping cream

Place the gingernut biscuits in a food processor and blitz to the consistency of fine breadcrumbs. Set aside. Line a baking sheet with cling film.

Put the vanilla seeds, mascarpone, caster sugar and cream into a bowl and whisk until smooth.

Place four 7 x 3.5cm deep metal chef's rings onto the lined baking sheet. Pipe or spoon the mixture into the rings and smooth off with a pallet knife. Cover with cling film and chill in the fridge for 4 hours until set.

Remove the clingfilm from the top of the cheesecakes. Spread the biscuit crumbs onto a plate and dip the top and bottom of the cheesecakes into the gingernut crumbs. Heat the sides of the metal rings with a blowtorch or hot cloth and slide the rings off. Transfer the cheesecakes to serving plates.

POACHED PEACHES

There is nothing better than poached peaches with a dollop of mascarpone. They also taste great served with ice cream and chopped nuts. You can use nectarines for this dessert, too.

Serves 4

4 large, ripe peaches
425ml red wine **(merlot)**
100g soft brown sugar
1 vanilla pod
4 tablespoons mascarpone

Boil the kettle and fill a large bowl with iced water. Place the peaches in a bowl and pour over enough boiling water to cover. Leave for 30 seconds, then remove with a slotted spoon and plunge into the bowl of iced water. Remove from the iced water and slip off the skins.

Pour the wine, brown sugar and vanilla pod into a pan that will accommodate the peaches snugly. Bring the wine to the boil, add the peaches, cover and simmer over a low heat for 10–15 minutes until tender but not soft. Turn the peaches halfway through cooking.

Remove the peaches from the pan and set aside to cool slightly, then cut each in half and remove the stones. Return the pan to the heat and boil the syrup for 8 minutes until reduced by half.

Spoon the peaches into bowls, pour over the syrup and serve each with a spoonful of mascarpone.

CHOCOLATE TRUFFLE POTS

Easy and quick to make – a chocolate hit that's fit for any occasion.

Serves 4

- 125g good-quality dark chocolate, minimum 70% cocoa solids, broken into pieces
- 125g milk chocolate, broken into pieces
- ¼ teaspoon instant coffee granules
- ½ teaspoon brandy
- 250ml whipping cream

Melt the dark and milk chocolate together in a heatproof bowl placed over a saucepan of gently simmering water. Stir until combined. Remove the bowl from the heat and set aside to cool slightly.

Put the brandy in an egg cup or very small bowl. Add the coffee and stir until dissolved. Whisk the cream until soft and velvety. (Do not fully whisk.)

Using a large metal spoon, gently fold the cream and the coffee mixture into the cooled, melted chocolate. Spoon the mixture into four ramekins. Chill for 4–6 hours.

Remove from the fridge an hour before serving and serve at room temperature.

CHOCOLATE BAVAROIS

A blast from the past – a pure piece of retro chocolateyness.

Serves 4

oil for greasing
2 gelatine leaves **(bronze leaf)**
2 free-range eggs, **separated**
40g caster sugar
385ml whipping cream
50g good-quality milk or dark
chocolate, **broken into pieces**

Lightly oil 4 x 150ml pudding basins. Soak the gelatine leaves in a little cold water for 4–5 minutes until soft.

In a mixing bowl, whisk the egg yolks and sugar together until light and fluffy. Pour 200ml of the cream into a saucepan and bring almost to the boil. Pour the warm cream into the egg mixture, stirring. Pour the mixture into a clean pan and cook over a low heat, stirring, until the mixture starts to thicken. Continue to stir gently until the mixture is thick enough to coat the back of the spoon. (Do not allow to boil or the mixture will curdle.)

Squeeze all the water out of the gelatine leaves and add them to the custard mixture. Stir until the gelatine has dissolved.

Pass the custard through a fine sieve into a bowl containing the chocolate pieces. Stir well until the chocolate has melted. Place the bowl in a larger bowl of iced water to cool.

Whisk the remaining cream to soft peaks and using a large metal spoon, fold into the chocolate mixture. Whisk the egg whites until they form soft peaks and fold into the chocolate mixture.

Pour the mixture into the prepared pudding basins and chill for 3–4 hours until set.

To serve, briefly dip the basins in hot water. Carefully loosen the sides of the bavarois and turn out onto serving plates.

CHOCOLATE FONDANTS

This is my all-time favourite recipe; if I see a fondant on any restaurant dessert menu, I have to order it. A runny centre is a must and, for that retro, black forest gâteau taste, serve with vanilla cream and cherries with kirsch.

Serves 4

125g good-quality dark chocolate, **minimum 70% cocoa solids**

125g unsalted butter, **cut into small pieces, plus extra for greasing**

4 free-range eggs

75g caster sugar

50g self-raising flour, **plus extra for dusting**

Melt the chocolate and butter together in a heatproof bowl placed over a saucepan of gently simmering water. Stir until combined then leave to cool.

Preheat the oven to 180°C / 350°F / gas mark 4. Lightly butter and flour 6 x 200ml pudding basins or dariole moulds. Whisk the eggs and sugar together until light and pale and doubled in volume.

Fold the egg mixture into the cooled chocolate. Sift in the flour and, using a large metal spoon, fold until combined.

Spoon the chocolate mixture into the prepared basins or moulds and bake for 8–9 minutes until risen – the key is to have a runny centre. Loosen around each fondant with a knife and carefully turn out onto serving plates.

CHOCOLATE AND ALMOND TORTE

A rich treat that will keep you coming back for more. This tastes delicious with rum and raisin ice cream or, if you're freeling a little healthier, a dollop of crème fraîche.

Serves 4–6

250g good-quality dark chocolate, minimum 70% cocoa solids

250g unsalted butter, cut into small pieces, plus extra for greasing

6 free-range eggs, separated

125g caster sugar

50g ground almonds

Preheat the oven to 190°C/350°F/gas mark 5. Lightly grease a 23-cm springform cake tin. Melt the chocolate and butter together in a heatproof bowl placed over a saucepan of gently simmering water. Stir until combined then leave to cool.

Whisk the egg yolks with the sugar until light and fluffy. Gradually pour the melted chocolate into the egg mixture, stirring constantly. Using a large spoon, fold in the ground almonds.

Put the egg whites into a clean dry bowl and whisk until they form stiff peaks. Using a large metal spoon, fold the egg whites into the chocolate mixture until they are just combined. Pour the mixture into the prepared tin and bake for 35 minutes. The torte will be very moist in the middle but resist cooking it for longer.

Remove the torte from the oven and leave to cool completely in the tin.

CUSTARD TART

You either love or hate custard tart. I love it and this recipe always hits the spot. For that ultimate brulée tart, sprinkle with caster sugar and caramelise the top.

Serves 4–6

- 1 x 20cm sweet pastry shell or 1 x 300g packet sweet pastry
- 500ml whipping cream
- 6 egg yolks
- 60g caster sugar
- ½ teaspoon freshly grated nutmeg

If using packet sweet pastry, preheat the oven to 200°C/400°F/gas mark 6. Lightly flour the work surface and roll out the pastry to a 30cm circle, 0.5cm thick. Use to line a deep-sided, 20cm loose-based tart tin.

Line the pastry with a sheet of baking parchment and fill with baking beans. Bake for 20 minutes. Take the tart shell from the oven and remove the parchment paper and beans. Reduce the oven temperature (or if you are using a sweet pastry shell, preheat the oven) to 150°C/300°F/gas mark 2.

Pour the cream into a pan and bring to a simmer. Remove from the heat and set aside.

In a large bowl, whisk the eggs yolks with the sugar until thick, creamy and pale in colour. Pour the simmered cream over the egg mixture and whisk together. Pass the mixture through a fine sieve into the prepared pastry shell or case. Sprinkle the grated nutmeg over the top of the tart. Bake for 1 hour until just set. The tart should be golden on the top with a slight tremor in the centre when you jiggle the tin.

Remove from the oven and leave to cool at room temperature on a wire rack. When cool, chill in the fridge until ready to serve.

CRÈME BRULÉE

A classic set custard with a crisp sugar top. I've adapted my big brother Chris' recipe, and it's the best brulée you will try!

Serves 4

1 large vanilla pod
250ml full-fat milk
250ml whipping cream
5 free-range egg yolks
100g caster sugar, **plus 8** tablespoons for the topping

Preheat the oven to 110°C/225°F/gas mark ½. Cut the vanilla pod in half lengthways and use the tip of a knife to scrape out the seeds into a saucepan. Put the vanilla pod and the milk in the pan. Place over a low heat and heat until just simmering. Remove from the heat.

In a bowl, whisk the eggs yolks with the sugar until pale and creamy, then slowly whisk in the warm milk and cream. Pass through a fine sieve and skim off any bubbles from the top.

Place four 'sur le plat' dishes (these are shallow, 10cm diameter dishes with crimped or winged edges) on a baking sheet. Divide the mixture between the four dishes. Place in the oven and cook for 1 hour. Remove from the oven and leave to cool, then chill in the fridge for 2–3 hours until set.

Sprinkle 2 tablespoons of caster sugar over each dish and shake the dish gently to spread the sugar evenly. Using a cook's blowtorch, hold the flame just above the surface and keep moving it round until the sugar is caramelised. Serve when the brulée is firm, or within an hour or two.

TIP
Don't be tempted to use deep ramekins – you need to use shallow dishes for this brulée.

ORANGE PANNACOTTA

So simple to make and quite delicious, especially when served with poached or fresh fruit salad. You can garnish with a little extra orange zest, if you like.

Serves 4

2 gelatine leaves (bronze leaf)
100ml full-fat milk
400ml whipping cream
zest of 1 orange
50g caster sugar

Soak the gelatine leaves in a little cold water for 4–5 minutes until soft. Pour the milk into a saucepan with the cream and orange zest and bring to the boil. Remove from the heat and add the sugar. Stir until dissolved.

Squeeze all the water out of the gelatine leaves and add them to the pan. Stir until the gelatine has dissolved. Pass through a fine sieve.

Divide the mixture among four 125ml dariole moulds, ramekins or teacups and leave to cool. Chill in the fridge for 2–3 hours until set.

Dip the moulds into hot water for 10 seconds each, then invert onto plates.

TIP
For a minty aftertone, add 6 fresh mint leaves to the saucepan with the cream and orange zest.

ROASTED HAZELNUT TART

The combination of maple syrup and hazelnuts is really moreish, so be careful not to munch too much of this sweet treat! Serve warm with clotted cream.

Serves 4

1 x 20cm sweet pastry shell or
   1 x 300g packet sweet
   pastry
250g hazelnuts
50g unsalted butter
3 large free-range eggs,
   lightly beaten
300ml maple syrup

Preheat the oven to 180°C/350°F/gas mark 4. Place the hazelnuts in a roasting tray and roast for 10 minutes until the skins become crisp and the nuts are beginning to brown. Remove from the oven and turn out onto a clean tea towel. Rub together in the tea towel to loosen and remove the skins (discard the skins). Set aside to cool.

Turn up the oven to 200°C/400°F/gas mark 6. If using a packet of sweet pastry, lightly flour the work surface and roll out the pastry to a 30cm circle, 0.5cm thick. Use to line a fluted, 20-cm loose-based tart tin. Tip the hazelnuts into the pastry case or shell.

Melt the butter in a pan over a low heat. Remove from the heat and beat in the eggs and maple syrup. Pour over the hazelnuts. Bake for 45 minutes until golden. Leave to cool in the tin.

CHOUX PASTRY

You like éclairs? Profiteroles? Choux buns? Then this is the perfect recipe for you. Use my crème pâtissière (page 173) as a filling and top with fondant icing or chocolate.

Serves 4, makes 12 choux buns or 8 éclairs

225ml water
110g butter
225g plain flour, sifted
5 free-range eggs, lightly beaten

Preheat the oven to 200°C/400°F/gas mark 6. Line a baking sheet with baking parchment. Pour the water into a saucepan with the butter. Cover the top of the saucepan with cling film and bring to the boil. Remove the cling film and add the flour quickly in one go.

Remove the pan from the heat and quickly beat the mixture vigorously to a firm paste, stirring continuously. Transfer the mixture to a bowl and leave to cool for 10 minutes.

Beat in the eggs (either by hand or using a mixer) a little at a time, stirring vigorously until the paste is smooth and glossy. Continue adding the egg until you have a soft dropping consistency.

Spoon the mixture into a large piping bag fitted with a plain nozzle and pipe the mixture onto the lined baking sheet as required. For choux buns pipe the mixture into 6cm discs or, for éclairs, pipe the mixture into sausage shapes 12cm in length.

Bake for 25–30 minutes until golden brown. Remove from the oven and transfer to a wire rack to cool. Fill the choux pastry with crème pâtissière (see page 173) or vanilla cream. Top with melted chocolate or fondant icing.

THE LIGHTEST SPONGE WITH RASPBERRIES & CREAM

This sponge is seriously light. It's up to you what to sandwich in the middle. As the sponge itself is low in fat, I thought I would make up for that by having my favourite filling – raspberries and cream!

Serves 4

vegetable oil, for greasing
4 large free-range eggs, separated
175g caster sugar, **plus extra for dredging**
150g self-raising flour, **sifted**
pinch of crushed sea salt
150ml whipping cream
225g raspberries

Preheat the oven to 180°C/ 350°F/gas mark 4. Grease and line two 20cm sponge tins with baking parchment.

In a mixing bowl, whisk the egg yolks and sugar together until pale and creamy. In a separate bowl, whisk the egg whites until stiff. Whisk the egg whites into the egg yolk mixture.

Fold in the flour in small batches using a large metal spoon. Repeat until all the flour is combined. Fold in the salt.

Divide the mixture between the two lined tins and bake for 20 minutes until well risen and golden. Remove from the oven, turn out onto a wire rack and leave to cool.

For the filling, pass 75g of the raspberries through a fine sieve. Set aside. Whip the cream to soft peaks and spread over one of the cooled sponges. Spoon the remaining raspberries over the cream and drizzle over the raspberry purée.

Top with the remaining cooled sponge and dredge with caster sugar. Serve with a cup of tea!

DOUGHNUTS

Eat these warm and try with different fillings: crème pâtissière, custard, jam, chocolate... I bet you'll be licking your fingers!

Serves 4

250g plain flour, plus extra for dusting

pinch crushed sea salt

90g caster sugar

25g cold butter, cut into small pieces

20g fresh yeast (from the bakery counter in the supermarket)

150ml warm full-fat milk

700ml oil for frying, plus extra for greasing

Sift the flour into a mixing bowl with the salt and 40g of the caster sugar. Rub the butter into the dry ingredients until it resembles fine breadcrumbs.

Put the yeast in a separate bowl with the warm milk and mix until the yeast is dissolved. Add the yeast mixture to the dry ingredients and using your hands, mix to a soft dough. (The dough will seem wet; leave it to stand for 10 minutes, after which it will have firmed a little.)

Turn the dough onto a lightly floured surface and knead for 5 minutes. Return the dough to the mixing bowl, cover with a damp tea towel and leave to prove in a warm place for 40 minutes until doubled in size.

Knock back the dough. Divide into 16 pieces and roll into small balls. Leave to prove on a lightly floured surface, covered with greased clingfilm, for 40 minutes until doubled in size.

Heat the oil in a saucepan to 180°C, or until a cube of bread dropped in turns golden in 30 seconds. Add the doughnuts, a few at a time, and deep fry for 2–3 minutes, turning occasionally until golden brown. (Make sure the oil is not too hot otherwise the doughnuts will brown in a second and not be cooked inside). Carefully remove the doughnuts with a slotted spoon and drain on kitchen paper. Continue to cook the rest in batches.

Sprinkle the remaining caster sugar onto a tray and roll the doughnuts in the sugar until coated. Serve warm.

AFTERNOON SCONES

I have always been a fan of the cream tea experience, so here is a great scone recipe. Just add tea, clotted cream and good-quality strawberry jam for the full monty.

Serves 4, makes 12 scones

oil for greasing
450g self-raising flour
3 teaspoons baking powder
pinch of crushed sea salt
75g cold butter, cut into cubes
50g caster sugar
225ml full-fat milk, plus extra
    for brushing

Lightly grease a baking sheet with oil. Sift the flour, baking powder and salt into a mixing bowl. Add the butter and rub into the flour until it resembles fine breadcrumbs. Stir in the sugar, then add the milk, a little at a time, to form a soft dough.

Lightly knead the dough on a floured surface and roll out to about 2.5cm in thickness. Using a 6cm pastry cutter, cut out 8 rounds and place on the greased baking sheet. Chill in the fridge for 20 minutes.

Preheat the oven to 200°C/400°F/gas mark 6. Brush the tops of the scones with a little milk and bake for 12–15 minutes until light and golden brown. Remove from the oven and cool on a wire rack.

TIP
For the perfect cheese scones, replae the 50g sugar with a pinch of sugar and add a handful of good-quality grated cheddar cheese into the mixture.

Breads & Sauces

For my breads, I always use fresh yeast, which is available at the bakery counter of any good supermarket (or ask your local bakery), but remember to keep the yeast in the fridge. There are some all-time sweet and savoury classic sauces in here too.

RUSTIC BREAD

I came up with this recipe years ago and still make it today. Serve with dipping pots of extra virgin olive oil and aged balsamic vinegar.

Makes 1 large family loaf
(approx. 1.5kg)

350ml water
200ml full-fat milk
15g caster sugar
25g fresh yeast
900g strong white flour, sifted, plus extra for dusting
25g crushed sea salt, plus 1 teaspoon
2 fresh rosemary sprigs
1 tablespoon olive oil

Pour the water and milk into a pan with the sugar and heat over a low heat until warm. Add the yeast and stir until dissolved.

Tip the flour into a mixing bowl with 25g of the salt. Pour over the yeast mixture. Using your hands, mix to a soft dough. (It may need a little more or less water, depending on how dry your flour is. The dough should be soft, but not sticky. If it is sticky, mix in a little extra flour.)

Turn the dough out onto a lightly floured surface and knead for 5 minutes. Return the dough to a floured mixing bowl, cover with a clean tea towel and leave in a warm place to prove for 40 minutes (or at room temperature for 1 hour) until doubled in size. Line a baking sheet with parchment paper.

Knock back the dough and form into a large rectangular shape around 5cm thick. Place the loaf on the lined baking sheet. Cover with a clean towel and leave in a warm place for 40 minutes (or at room temperature for 1 hour) until doubled in size. Preheat the oven to 200°C/400°F/gas mark 6.

Using the tips of your fingers, make dents all over the loaf. Pick the leaves off the rosemary sprigs and push into the loaf. Drizzle with the olive oil and sprinkle with the remaining teaspoon of crushed sea salt.

Bake for 30–35 minutes until well risen and golden. Turn out and check it is cooked by tapping the base; it should sound hollow. Leave to cool on a wire rack.

TANNER'S WHOLEMEAL BREAD

A brilliant easy-to-make wholemeal loaf. Enjoy with good-quality butter or, even better, use to make the ultimate fresh crab sarnie!

Makes 2 x 900g loaves

425ml warm water

50ml olive oil, plus extra for
 greasing

25g fresh yeast

15g soft light brown sugar

450g strong white flour, plus
 extra for dusting

450g brown flour

1 teaspoon crushed sea salt

Pour the warm water into a mixing bowl with the olive oil. Add the yeast and sugar and whisk until the sugar has dissolved.

Tip the strong white and brown flour into a second mixing bowl with the salt. Pour over the yeast mixture and, using your hands, mix to a soft dough. (It may need a little more or less water, depending on how dry your flour is. The dough should be soft, but not sticky. If it is sticky, mix in a little extra flour.)

Turn the dough onto a lightly floured surface and knead for 10 minutes.

Return the dough to the mixing bowl, cover with a clean tea towel and leave in a warm place to prove for 40 minutes (or at room temperature for 1 hour) until doubled in size. Grease 2 x 900g loaf tins with olive oil.

Knock back the dough and form into 2 loaves. Place in the greased tins, pressing firmly all around the edges so that the loaves are slightly rounded. Cover with a clean towel and leave in a warm place for 40 minutes (or at room temperature for 1 hour) until doubled in size. Preheat the oven to 200°C/400°F/gas mark 6.

Bake the loaves for 35–40 minutes, until well risen and golden. Turn out and check they are cooked by tapping on their bases; they should sound hollow. Leave to cool on a wire rack.

SUNDRIED TOMATO CIABATTA

This takes the longest time to make of the breads in this book, but is well worth the wait. Experiment with flavours for this recipe – fresh herbs, pitted olives, marinated artichokes – which you would add at the same time as the tomatoes.

Makes 3 ciabatta loaves

for the starter

10g fresh yeast

175ml warm water

350g strong plain flour, **plus extra for dusting**

for the dough

400ml warm water

60ml warm full-fat milk

15g fresh yeast

500g strong plain flour

115g (drained weight) sundried tomatoes, **chopped**

2 teaspoons salt

3 tablespoons olive oil

For the starter, cream the yeast with 3 tablespoons of the water. Tip the flour into a mixing bowl. Gradually mix in the yeast mixture and the remaining water to form a firm dough.

Turn the dough onto a lightly floured surface and knead for 5 minutes until smooth and elastic. Return to the bowl. Cover with lightly oiled cling film and leave in a warm place for 12–15 hours, until the dough has risen and started to collapse. Dust three baking sheets with flour.

For the dough, pour the warm water and warm milk into a mixing bowl. Add the yeast and whisk until dissolved. Add the yeast liquid to the starter mixture and mix together. Using your hands, gradually add the flour, lifting the dough as you mix. (This will take about 10 minutes). Add the chopped tomatoes, salt and olive oil. Cover the bowl with lightly oiled cling film and leave in a warm place to prove for 1 to 1½ hours until doubled in size.

Rub your hands with some flour, tip one-third of the dough onto a baking sheet, trying to avoid knocking back the dough. Shape into a rectangle, 2.5cm thick. Dust lightly with flour. Repeat with the remaining dough to make a further 2 loaves. Leave in a warm place for 30 minutes.

Preheat the oven to 220°C/425°F/gas mark 7. Bake the ciabatta for 25–30 minutes until golden brown. Slide off the baking sheets and check they are cooked by tapping their bases; they should sound hollow. Leave to cool on a wire rack.

TOMATO AND OLIVE BREAD

This bread is great eaten as it is and even tastier when used to make crostini or bruschetta.

Makes 2 x 750g loaves

150ml warm water

50ml olive oil, plus extra for greasing

25g fresh yeast

15g caster sugar

900g strong white flour, plus extra for dusting

15g crushed sea salt

250ml tomato juice

100g (handful) pitted black olives

Pour the warm water into a mixing bowl. Add the olive oil, yeast and sugar and whisk until the yeast has dissolved.

Tip the flour into a second mixing bowl with the salt. Pour over the yeast mixture and the tomato juice. Using your hands, mix to a soft dough. (It may need a little more or less water, depending on how dry your flour is. The dough should be soft, but not sticky. If it is sticky, mix in a little extra flour.)

Turn the dough onto a lightly floured surface and knead for 10 minutes, adding the olives a few at a time. Return the dough to the mixing bowl, cover with a clean tea towel and leave in a warm place to prove for 40 minutes (or at room temperature for 1 hour) until doubled in size. Grease 2 x 900g loaf tins with olive oil, or flour 2 baking sheets.

Knock back the dough and form into 2 loaves. Place in the greased tins or shape and place on the floured baking sheets. Cover with a clean tea towel and leave on a warm place for 40 minutes (or at room temperature for 1 hour) until doubled in size. Preheat the oven to 200°C/400°F/gas mark 6.

Dust the loaves lightly with flour. Bake for 25–30 minutes, until well risen and golden. Turn out and check they are cooked by tapping on their bases. They should sound hollow. Leave to cool on a wire rack.

FRESH MAYONNAISE

Why buy mayonnaise when this recipe takes minutes to make and tastes great! It is best used immediately so don't store in the fridge for more than 24 hours.

Makes 300ml

2 medium free-range
egg yolks
1 teaspoon dijon mustard
250ml light olive oil
juice of ½ lemon
crushed sea salt and freshly
ground black pepper

Sit a large mixing bowl on a tea towel to prevent it moving around. Place the egg yolks in the bowl with the mustard, a pinch of sea salt and freshly ground black pepper.

Using a large balloon whisk or electric hand whisk, whisk the ingredients together. Gradually add the oil in a slow, steady stream, whisking continuously until you have a smooth thick mayonnaise.

Check the seasoning and whisk in the lemon juice.

For a thinner mayonnaise, whisk in a couple of drops of boiling water with the lemon juice.

TARTARE SAUCE

This sauce is perfect with any fish, so use it with my Beer Battered Fish (see page 60)!

Makes 300ml

1 quantity of mayonnaise
   (see opposite)
3 tablespoons cornichons (baby
   gherkins), drained and finely
   chopped
2 tablespoons capers, drained
   and finely chopped
1 shallot, finely chopped
3 tablespoons, fresh flat-leaf
   parsley, chopped
crushed sea salt and freshly
   ground black pepper

Place the mayonnaise in a mixing bowl. Add the cornichons, capers, shallot and parsley and mix together. Season to taste with crushed sea salt and freshly ground black pepper.

Serve immediately if using the fresh mayonnaise opposite. If you're using shop-bought mayonnaise store, covered, in the fridge for up to 4 days.

SALSA VERDE

The king of salsas: packed with fresh flavours and it works with just about anything!

Serves 4

40g (large handful) fresh flat-leaf parsley leaves

20g (small handful) fresh basil or mint leaves

zest and juice of 1 lemon

1 garlic clove, **crushed**

3 anchovy fillets, **chopped**

120ml extra virgin olive oil

crushed sea salt and freshly ground black pepper

Wash the parsley, basil or mint leaves, shake, then pat dry with kitchen paper. Pour the lemon juice and zest into the bowl of a food processor. Add the herbs and blitz using the pulse action to make a very coarse paste (don't overprocess).

Add the garlic and anchovies and blitz, again using the pulse action to achieve a coarse paste.

With the motor running, gradually add the extra virgin olive oil. Remove from the bowl and transfer into a mixing bowl. Season to taste with crushed sea salt and freshly ground black pepper. Cover with cling film and chill in the fridge until needed. Use within 24 hours.

CUSTARD

The ultimate crème anglaise or should I say English custard!? This is proper custard –it's not thick and gloopy but coats the back of a spoon – and it's much easier to make than people think.

Serves 4, makes 600ml

1 vanilla pod
500ml full-fat milk
6 free-range egg yolks
100g caster sugar

Cut the vanilla pod in half lengthways and use the tip of a knife to scrape out the seeds into a saucepan. Put the vanilla pod and the milk in the pan. Place over a low heat until just simmering. Remove from the heat and set aside.

Whisk the eggs yolks with the sugar until light and creamy. Pour the warm milk over the egg mixture, stirring. Pour the mixture into a clean pan and cook over a very low heat, stirring constantly, until the mixture starts to thicken. (Be careful not to let the mixture boil or it will split.) Stir gently until the mixture is thick enough to coat the back of the spoon. Remove from the heat and pass through a fine sieve.

Pour the custard into a jug or bowl to serve.

CRÈME PÂTISSIÈRE

Crème pâtissière is simply confectioner's custard: thick, rich and creamy. It's a useful filling for many sweet pastries, such as choux pastry, mille-feuille, doughnuts and Danish pastries.

Serves 4, makes 600ml

1 vanilla pod
600ml full-fat milk
6 free-range egg yolks
75g caster sugar
50g plain flour

Cut the vanilla pod in half lengthways and use the tip of a knife to scrape out the seeds into a saucepan. Put the vanilla pod and the milk in the pan. Place over a low heat and heat until just simmering. Remove from the heat and set aside.

Whisk the eggs yolks with the sugar until light and creamy. Pour the warm milk over the egg mixture, stirring. Pour the mixture into a clean pan and cook over a low heat for 4–5 minutes, whisking, until the mixture starts to thicken and the whisk leaves a trail in the custard (the mixture should be thick and the flour taste cooked out).

Remove from the heat and pass through a fine sieve before serving. If you're not using immediately, cover the surface with cling film to prevent a skin forming. Cool to room temperature and store in the fridge for up to 48 hours.

INDEX